Contents

Contents

Butterflies
of Berkshire Buckinghamshire & Oxfordshire

Caroline and David Steel
Illustrated by Peter Creed

Pisces
PUBLICATIONS

Illustrations © Pisces Publications 1985, except pp. 47–52, 56, 60, 63 and
65, reproduced courtesy of Penguin Books Limited. First published in Atlas of
Butterflies in Britain and Ireland by Heath, Pollard and Thomas, Viking 1984.

First published 1985 by Pisces Publications, Brasenose Farm, Eastern By-pass,
Oxford.

British Library Cataloguing in Publication Data

Steel, Caroline
    Butterflies of Berkshire, Buckinghamshire & Oxfordshire.
    1. Butterflies—England—Midlands
    I. Title II. Steel, David, 1951-
    III. Creed, Peter
    595.78'9'09425   QL555.G7
    ISBN 0 0508216 3 4

Designed by Pisces Publications
Printed by Holywell Press Ltd., Alfred Street, Oxford.

Preface

Why write a book on the butterflies of Berkshire, Buckinghamshire and Oxfordshire? Although there have been several publications which include information on this topic[1-4], no comprehensive guide has ever been produced in a form accessible to the general public. There can be few better places to become familiar with our British butterflies with 49 out of the 63 regularly breeding British species. The broad aim of this publication is to provide information which will allow a greater appreciation of this precious resource.

We hope to give both the interested layman and the butterfly enthusiast a better knowledge of the region's butterflies. The colour plates and descriptions will be a valuable aid to identification and should allow beginners to become familiar with all of the butterflies likely to be encountered. The distribution maps provide a statement on the status of the region's butterflies over the period 1975 – 84. A glance at these maps will give some cause for concern because several species are now confined to a handful of sites, and without active conservation measures some are likely to disappear over succeeding decades. Finally, we have indicated areas where we have very little information and it is our hope that this publication will encourage further recording and study of butterflies.

Acknowledgements

A great many people provided records of one sort or another, and we would like to express our thanks to M. Adams, M. Albertini, J. Asher, B. Baker of the Berkshire Museum, M. Barnsley, the British Butterfly Conservation Society, The Berkshire, Buckinghamshire and Oxfordshire Naturalists' Trust, G. Bellamy, the Biological Records Centre, P. Bond, P. Boston, H. Bowen, N. Bowles, J. Campbell of the Oxfordshire Museum, P. Cawdell, W. Churchill, M. Corley, P. Creed, V. Darbyshire, R. Edwards, P. Ford, C. Gibson, M. Goddard, D. Gore, E. Gow, T. Grout-Smith, J. Hall, J. Hannah, P. Hayter, S. Hiscock, R. Hornby, M. Hughes, I. Johnston, R. Kemp, A. Kennard, R. Knight, J. Laker, R. Louch, E. MacDean, P. Marren, M. Marsh, J. Martin, K. Merrifield, J. Milton, the Nature Conservancy Council, J. Norledge, M. Oates, C. Ormonde, G. Osmond, N. Phillips, K. Porter, D. Read, D. Redhead, J. Searle, J. Royston of The Buckinghamshire Museum, A. Showler, R. Smith, A. Strong, J. Trotman, J. Tyler, A. Ward-Smith, D. Wedd, M. Wemyss, M. Wigan, B. Wildridge, M. Wilkins, T. Williams, J. Wise, G. Wynne-Thomas, and R. Youngman.

We would like to express our thanks to JRJ Advertising for their financial support and to Mrs Gwenneth Steel for her skill in typing the various drafts.

Caroline and David Steel,
Oxford, March 1985.

Introduction

There are many indications of the growing popularity of butterflies with the British people. Many of the high quality television films about the British countryside include sections on butterflies, and there has been a profusion of butterfly books published over the past decade, including The Atlas of Butterflies in Britain and Ireland[5], published in 1984. 1981 – 82 was designated 'Butterfly Year' which commenced with an issue of postage stamps of British butterflies and which resulted in much mass media publicity for butterflies. A number of butterfly houses have since been established where the public is able to walk amongst free-flying butterflies.

It is easy to understand why butterflies are so popular. Their movement, great beauty and brilliance of colour add gaiety to the garden and countryside. There are many fascinating aspects of butterfly behaviour which make for interesting watching. Several species have elaborate courtship displays, some butterflies will aggressively defend their territory and most species are capable of astonishingly effective camouflage when at rest. Some species are easy to rear and many people obtain great pleasure from observing the changing from caterpillar into chrysalis, and then into a perfect butterfly. In Victorian times butterfly collecting was a popular pastime, but fortunately, few people wish to kill and collect butterflies nowadays. The camera is fast replacing the collecting net, with the collection of slides or photographs replacing the collection of pinned specimens. The onset of reasonably priced 'single lens reflex' cameras has enabled the amateur to produce excellent quality photographs of butterflies. A complete set of the British butterflies on film is just as challenging and rewarding as a complete set of the butterflies themselves. Although there is little evidence that collecting did any long term damage to butterfly populations, the movement towards the use of the camera rather than the net is undoubtedly a welcome step forward.

However, the main reason for the increased interest over the past decade results from the heightened awareness of dramatic changes which are taking place in our countryside and their associated adverse effects on wildlife. Surveys by entomologists throughout Britian have confirmed that most of our butterflies are undergoing a severe decline. Indeed two species, the large blue and chequered skipper, have recently become extinct. The chequered skipper had disappeared from all its English localities by 1976, and in 1979 the large blue was declared extinct in Britain. Modern methods of farming and forestry, and the increase in urbanisation have both caused the destruction and alteration of habitats – with a resulting decline in butterfly populations. Massive local extinctions have occurred particularly in the eastern counties of England and nearly twenty species have shown a major contraction in range during the last forty years. Many other species have declined in abundance within their ranges. The three counties of Berkshire, Buckinghamshire and Oxfordshire have not escaped these declines, but have become particularly important in that they still support a number of species which no longer occur to the east of the region. However, as the distribution maps show, most of these species are extremely local and some only exist at a handful of sites. Consequently, we hope that this publication will add to the growing realisation that we are likely to lose more of our butterflies unless adequate conservation measures are taken.

Life cycle

If asked 'What is a butterfly?' most children would know that it is an insect. However, they would not understand the intricacies of a butterfly's life cycle – essential for a full understanding of their behaviour and ecology. There are alternative names for the life cycle stages and those that are used in the text are italicised, with the alternatives following in parentheses. *Adults* (imagos) lay their *eggs* (ova) on or near the *larval* (caterpillar's) foodplant. Larvae have several (usually 4 or 5) *instars* (stages) and after each one they cease feeding and burst out of the old skin. The new skin underneath is larger than the old one, to allow for growth, and may be differently coloured. Eventually the fully mature larva changes into a *pupa* (chrysalis) which can be either attached to the foodplant or to a substrate nearby. The pupa metamorphoses into an adult butterfly, so completing the life cycle.

Most butterflies have one *brood* (generation) a year and the typical average life of an individual is only one or two weeks. However, as the butterflies do not always emerge on the same day – indeed males often emerge about a week earlier than females, the flight period of a particular species may extend for several weeks. Some species are double brooded, such as the adonis blue and brown argus, or even triple brooded such as the speckled wood. Occasionally, during exceptionally hot summers, a partial second brood may occur in a species which is normally single brooded. Examples can be found in such species as the wood white, small pearl-bordered fritillary and small blue. Usually only a few individuals are seen with these partial broods.

Identification

It is extremely easy to make mistakes when identifying butterflies, and beginners frequently believe they have seen such rare species as fritillaries or large tortoiseshells in their gardens. Although possible, these records are almost certainly misidentifications. Once familiar with a species, a trained eye will be able to identify it at a glance. However, until that time it is wisest to carry out a number of checks before identifying a butterfly.

Check the flight period Most butterflies have a short flight season and are unlikely to be seen outside this period. Brown hairstreak records from June, for example, will probably be errors because this butterfly flies in August and September.

Check the habitat requirements Many of the rare and local species are particular in their habitat requirements. Adonis blues, for example, require unimproved downland where the turf is well-grazed and contains horseshoe vetch. Hence any records from non-calcareous areas, or from downland which does not have horseshoe vetch, are likely to be mistaken – probably for the rather similar common blue.

Check the markings Careful attention to detail is essential when determining closely related species which have similar markings. Small and Essex skippers, and pearl-bordered and small pearl-bordered fritillaries for example, fly together and can only be distinguished after close observation.

A very small proportion of butterfles are abnormal in some way. These freaks are known as aberrations or variations and can cause problems of identification. The study and collection of aberrations was very popular in the past and rare specimens changed hands for considerable sums of money. In recent years interest in aberrations has diminished although there is still a small band of enthusiasts. However, these oddities are worth looking out for in the countryside. Well known examples include the greenish *valezina* form of the silver-washed fritillary (which only occurs in the female) and the all black *nigrina* form of the white admiral.

Although many of the region's butterflies may be identified from the colour illustrations in this book, additional help may be obtained from one of the many good books which are currently on the market[n]'. By far the easiest way to learn to identify butterflies is to join a society which provides guided walks led by experts. Details of two local societies are given on page 80. Whichever way you choose, the learning process can give a great deal of pleasure and satisfaction.

Where to see butterflies

Many readers will stray no further than their garden to watch butter-flies. As a large garden may support up to 20 species – nearly one third of the national total, what better place is there to become familiar with these charming insects? However, the butterfly enthusiast will wish to venture into the countryside in search of some of the more elusive species. The richest parts of our region support up to 42 species in each 10 kilometre (km) square and clearly short excursions in these areas should enable the reader to become familiar with most of the region's butterflies. There is a small number of sites accessible to the general public which are outstandingly rich in butterflies – for chalkland species visit Watlington Hill in Oxfordshire or Ivinghoe Beacon in Buckingham-shire; for heathland species visit Silchester Common on the Berkshire / Hampshire border; while Bernwood Forest on the Buckinghamshire / Oxfordshire border is famous for its profusion of woodland species. More information on favoured habitats is given in the species text, but details of good sites can only be gleaned by meeting other butterfly enthusiasts or by joining one of the local conservation societies. Sites with rare and endangered species are not named because collecting can still be a pro-blem where populations are very low, and a number of rarities occur on land which is strictly private.

Distribution

The distribution of the butterflies is shown by means of the 10 km squares on the British National Grid. Each shaded square represents at least a single record within the period 1975 – 84. There are 79 10 km squares and part squares covering the three counties and the map (Fig. 1) shows the number of species recorded in each square during this period. Errors on the map are much more likely to be ones of omission than of addition, because dubious records were as far as possible checked. The coverage was by no means even, and peripheral squares in particular, were under-recorded. However, the numbers recorded do broadly reflect the habitat quality and squares with high totals are the richest areas for butterflies.

48 or 49 species regularly breed in the three counties, but none of these are sufficiently endangered in Britain to be listed in the Wild Life and Countryside Act 1981. The region does however, possess several rare and very local species and these have been mapped accurately. It would prove difficult to locate a particular colony of butterflies within a 10 km square and so there should be no danger from unscrupulous collectors.

The simple geological map (Fig. 3) allows a comparison of butterfly distribution with geology. Species such as the silver-studded blue (shown on the distribution map Fig. 2) can be seen to be restricted to the London clay and tertiary gravels of Berkshire, whereas species such as the adonis blue and small blue, are confined to calcareous soils. One factor limiting the distribution of these species is the distribution of their larval foodplants. The silver-studded blue uses mainly heathers and gorse as larval foodplants, which only grow in abundance on acid heathlands. By contast, adonis blue larvae feed exclusively on horseshoe vetch which is a strict calcicole. Most of the commoner species such as the whites, peacock and hedge brown, show no preference for soil type – largely

Fig. 1 Numbers of species recorded in each 10km square

Fig. 2 Distribution of silver-studded blue

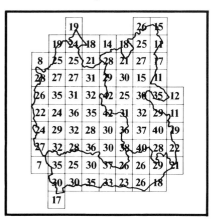

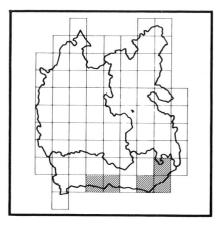

Fig. 3 Simplified geological map of Berkshire, Buckinghamshire and Oxfordshire

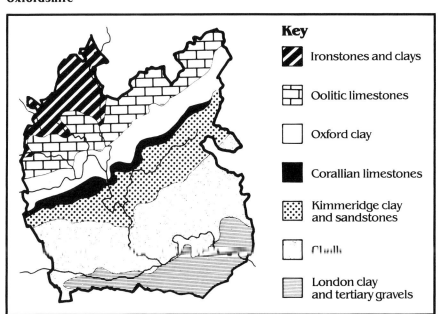

Key

Ironstones and clays

Oolitic limestones

Oxford clay

Corallian limestones

Kimmeridge clay and sandstones

Chalk

London clay and tertiary gravels

because they have ubiquitous larval foodplants.

Climate is another limiting factor and a number of species which have a southerly distribution in England, are here at the northern limits of their range. The adonis blue and silver-spotted skipper are good examples and tend to only breed on south-facing slopes where local conditions are hottest.

Changes in distribution and status

The aim of the maps is to show a clear picture of the current distribution of the region's butterflies. For the sake of clarity, pre-1975 records have not been included and readers should refer to the Atlas of Butterflies in Britain and Ireland[5] for a summary of past distributions. The Atlas of Oxfordshire Butterflies[24] also includes present and historic records which are mapped at tetrad (2km[2]) level.

Nevertheless historical information is essential for a full understanding of the changes in status of the different species, and where possible, such information has been included in the species texts which accompany the maps. Historical records have been gleaned from a number of publications[1-4, 16, 19, 20] supplemented by unpublished observations from several entomologists. However, in general, records from the past are rather patchy and many give little indication of status. A proposed publication on the Lepidoptera of Berkshire, and an update of the 'Macrolepidoptera of Buckinghamshire'[12], may eventually fill in some of these gaps.

Butterfly recording has been in progress for many years and each of the three counties has a biological records centre based at the county museums. The Oxfordshire museum now publishes regular records of the county's butterflies on a tetrad basis, and an extension of this system to all counties would enable changes in the distribution of our butterflies to be accurately monitored.

An assessment of the changes of status of the region's butterflies during the past 30 years shows that nearly 75% of the species have declined in numbers (see Table 1). Seven species are threatened with extinction, thirteen species have shown major declines and ten species, some of which could be classed as relatively common, have shown local declines within their range. Set against this there are four species which have increased their range. Most of these species have shown the same increases nationally which are in part responses to changes in habitat, and in part responses to small changes in climate.

Table 1   Changes in status of Butterflies in Berkshire, Buckinghamshire and Oxfordshire over the period 1955 – 84

EXTINCT SPECIES	THREATENED WITH EXTINCTION	MAJOR DECLINES	LOCAL DECLINES	INCREASES
Chequered skipper	Silver-spotted skipper Adonis blue Large tortoiseshell Small pearl-bordered fritillary Pearl-bordered fritillary High brown fritillary Marsh fritillary	Dingy skipper Grizzled skipper Brown hairstreak White-letter hairstreak Black hairstreak Small blue Silver-studded blue Brown argus Chalkhill blue Duke of Burgundy Dark green fritillary Silver-washed fritillary Grayling	Green-veined white Orange tip Green hairstreak Purple hairstreak Small copper Common blue Purple emperor Wall Small heath Ringlet	Essex skipper Wood white White admiral Comma
1 species	7 species	13 species	10 species	4 species

Conservation

Many people wish that butterflies could be more numerous in our countryside. To those fortunate enough to possess the memory of clouds of butterflies seen one summer's day, this vivid memory is likely to remain for ever.

The term *conservation* with respect to butterflies, means some kind of wise land management whereby sufficient suitable conditions are provided to support strong colonies of all our native butterflies. Every butterfly has precise environmental requirements. These requirements are crucial for the survival of each butterfly species. Hence, butterfly conservation is largely a question of providing the correct environmental conditions or habitat.

About 25% of the region's butterflies are able to live in relative harmony with the present systems of agriculture and forestry. The small tortoiseshell breeds well in the vicinity of farms and gardens; meadow browns occur on most sheltered grasslands, and speckled woods thrive in all woods except the most dense conifer plantations. Butterflies such as these are widespread in the three counties and seem likely to remain with us for the forseeable future.

The other 75% of the region's butterflies are much more specific in their habitat requirements. These butterflies require seminatural habitats, which are places where the flora and fauna is related more to the soil and climate than to the direct intervention of man. Examples of such species include the chalkhill blue which demands calcareous grassland; the purple emperor which demands extensive areas of woodland with goat willow; and the silver-studded blue which requires large areas of heathland. The fact that many of these butterflies are thinly scattered and decreasing in abundance is due to the paucity of suitable seminatural habitats and to the decline of their traditional management.

Habitat management

The following are essential requirements for all butterfly habitats: appropriate foodplants for the larvae; nectar, honeydew or other nutrient sources for the adults; and shelter from strong winds. Habitats can be managed in a variety of ways and for a variety of reasons. Some management operations are beneficial to butterflies while others are harmful.

Management operations certain to be damaging to butterfly habitats include ploughing of downland and heathland, applications of fertilizers and pesticides, woodland clearance and drainage of wet meadows. A large area of the Berkshire Downs has been ploughed and converted to arable farming, resulting in the loss of many colonies of chalkland species such as the adonis and chalkhill blues. In Berkshire, areas of heathland have been lost to building, gravel extraction and conifer plantations, so reducing the number of suitable breeding sites for heathland species such as the silver-studded blue and grayling. Large applications of pesticides will kill butterflies outright but the damaging effects of fertilizers are more insidious. Vigorous grass cultivars respond rapidly to fertilizers with the result that other herbaceous species and less vigorous grasses are unable to tolerate the new conditions. The latter group contains many larval foodplants and hence their loss will result in the extinction of associated butterflies. In north Buckinghamshire a number of woods have been total-ly cleared for agriculture, resulting in the loss of black hairstreak colonies and other woodland species. The drainage and improvement of marshy fields throughout the region will almost certainly have adversely affected the marsh fritillary. Such losses of seminatural habitat have been severe in all three counties (Table 2).

Another factor likely to be damaging to butterfly populations is the decline of traditional management of habitats. The cessation of grazing on downland and the decline of traditional woodland management tech-niques have both been partly responsible for losses of both grassland and woodland butterflies over the past thirty years. Traditional sheep grazing became less popular in the late 19th century, but during the period 1900 – 50, areas of grassland were often kept short by high rabbit popula-tions. However, the introduction of myxomatosis in the early 1950s had a dramatic effect on both rabbit and butterfly populations. With the loss of

Table 2 Habitat loss

Surveys by the Berkshire, Buckinghamshire and Oxfordshire Naturalists' Trust (BBONT)[22] in 1978 – 79 and 1981, showed that the total area of surviving seminatural habitat was less than ten percent of the total area of the three counties.

% of selected seminatural habitats in Berkshire, Buckinghamshire and Oxfordshire		
Habitat	Area (ha)	% of total area
Dry, calcareous grassland	3,639	0.63
Neutral grassland	5,570	0.97
Scrub	1,301	0.23
Woodland	38,827.5	6.75
Ancient woodland	2,945	0.51
Heathland	1,246	0.22
Wetland	1,324	0.23

The survey identified 513,659ha (=89.3%) of the three counties as being improved farmland or roads and houses – such areas are of limited value to wildlife. Even the woodland figure includes a percentage of coniferous plant-ations which again are of limited value for wildlife. This information is backed up by other sources. A 1983 survey by the Nature Conservancy Council[23] show-ed that 36% of Oxfordshire's ancient woodland had been lost or converted to plantation since 1930. The same source estimated that 95% of English neutral grasslands, including herb-rich hay meadows, now lack significant wildlife interest, and only 3% are unaffected by agricultural intensification.

rabbits, herb-rich downland soon became overgrown and important butterfly foodplants were choked out by coarser grasses and invading scrub. The loss of certain silver-spotted skipper and adonis blue colonies from the Chilterns can almost certainly be attributed to this factor[8]. Conversely, overgrazing of downland can be a problem and several local extinctions are known to have been caused in this way. The Duke of Burgundy requires large, flowering cowslip plants which are growing in slightly shaded conditions. Intensive grazing will suppress the growth of these plants, thereby making the habitat unsuitable for the butterfly. The small blue will likewise be affected, as its larvae feed in the flowerheads of kidney vetch. Heavy grazing during the flowering period will eliminate both flowers and butterfly.

Traditional woodland management involved operations such as coppicing, regular selective felling and ride maintenance, all of which resulted in substantial transient open areas within a wood. The cessation of operations such as these, as well as the replacement of broad-leaved trees with conifers, is probably responsible for the dramatic decline of woodland butterflies such as the pearl-bordered and high brown fritillaries. The loss of fritillaries has been documented at Ashridge wood in west Berkshire. In the 1930s and 40s good numbers of pearl-bordered and silver-washed fritillaries were recorded, as well as smaller numbers of high brown and small pearl-bordered fritillaries. The dark green fritillary occurred in a meadow just outside the wood. The fritillaries declined sharply in numbers in the late 1940s and had all disappeared by the early 1950s. A broadly similar pattern was observed at the nearby Catmore wood.

Few butterflies will survive the shady conditions of old neglected coppice or dense conifer plantations. However, a newly planted conifer plantation may support a number of species if the old woodland flora is still present. Indeed, at several sites in the region, a few of the rarer species appear to be thriving in such areas. The wood white, for example, is frequently encountered in young plantations in north Oxfordshire and Buckinghamshire. Unfortunately the benefits are only short term – after fifteen years or so the maturing conifers cast a good deal of shade and eventually suppress the vital nectar and larval foodplants. The rides, if wide enough, may support the butterflies for a short period, but in general most species will have disappeared before the trees are felled and a new area is opened up.

Commercial forestry and modern farming practices are therefore major threats to the survival of our butterflies. We have also seen that extremely low percentages of seminatural habitat remain in the three counties. Consequently, a number of butterflies with precise habitat requirements are now very scarce, and likely to become extinct in the near future unless adequate conservation measures are taken. Some of the best surviving examples of seminatural habitats in the region have been made into nature reserves, and a number of these are positively managed to encourage butterflies. BBONT manages over 80 reserves and has played an active part in the conservation of the black hairstreak, a rare species which breeds on a number of their reserves. The Nature Conservancy Council manages three National Nature Reserves in the region, including a large site in the Chilterns which has important populations of some of the rarer chalkland species. They also manage, jointly with the Forestry Commission, the Forest Nature Reserve in Bernwood Forest – a site of national importance for its woodland butterflies. Other protected areas include National Trust properties, country parks and Local Nature Reserves. Although a number of these places are not managed specifically for butterflies, they do provide important reservoirs of our butterfly fauna.

Nevertheless, protected areas represent less than 1% of the total area of the three counties. Of the species threatened with extinction (see Table 1), only three – the silver-spotted skipper, pearl-bordered fritillary and marsh fritillary, have viable colonies on nature reserves. Many colonies on nature reserves are threatened simply by their isolation. If the colony is small and prone to natural fluctuations, caused by parasites or bad weather, there is a high probability that the colony will eventually die out. Once such extinctions occur, the chance of natural recolonisation is very small. Even with the more mobile species, the hostile nature of modern agricultural land often precludes movement between colonies. Therefore, to ensure that populations remain large enough to make chance extinctions unlikely, an understanding of the butterflies' needs, together with a programme of sensitive management, is vital.

Butterfly gardening

One particular form of habitat management has become known as butterfly gardening. Most gardens will support up to ten species of butterfly, but appropriate measures may increase this number to about twenty.

The simplest way to attract butterfies to a garden is to provide a range of flowers which produce nectar throughout the butterfly year (March – October). There are several excellent books which give details on this topic[9-11], but well known butterfly plants include aubretia, buddleia, ice plant, michaelmas daisies and marigolds. These plants are certain to attract strong flying butterflies such as small tortoiseshells, red admirals, painted ladies and large whites.

A more ambitious way of encouraging butterflies is to grow a range of larval foodplants to enable butterflies to breed in the garden. If a section of lawn is allowed to grow long and cut only once a year in the autumn, grass feeding larvae of species such as large and small skippers, small heath, meadow brown and hedge brown will be encouraged. A patch of nettles in a sunny situation will provide a breeding place for several of the vanessid butterflies including small tortoiseshell, comma, peacock and red admiral. Clumps of ivy are valuable both as a larval foodplant for the holly blue and as a hibernating site for the brimstone. Larger gardens may accommodate foodplants such as hop, elm, buckthorn and cuckoo flower – in fact the possibilites are endless.

Many people are concerned about the increased use of pesticides in the garden. There is a great deal of media pressure to persuade the public that trouble-free gardening involves regular spraying operations. One result of pesticide applications is that gardens will become poorer in the number of butterflies. The conscientious butterfly gardener, for example, will always remove 'cabbage white' caterpillars by hand, rather than spray, or will sacrifice a small patch of *brassicas* in order to retain the pleasure of seeing these butterflies winging about the garden.

Butterfly ecology and monitoring

Considering the popularity of butterflies in Britain, there is surprisingly little detailed information on their ecology. Butterfly ecology, which is the study of the interrelationships between butterflies and their living and mineral surroundings, is both intrinsically interesting and likely to assist with the conservation of some of our rare species. The diligent amateur is able to make valuable contributions to our understanding of butterfly ecology. Examples of questions which might be answered include: Which nectar plants are visited by the different butterfly species? Which grasses are used by grass-feeding larvae? What changes of habitat are associated with the loss of fritillaries from our region? How do closely related species such as small/Essex skippers, pearl bordered/small pearl bordered fritillaries and dark green/high brown fritillaries coexist alongside each other? To what extent does the presence of a good range of butterflies at a site provide an indication of its overall 'ecological health'? Once started on a detailed study of butterflies many people find the work fascinating and it becomes a consuming interest for the rest of their life.

The monitoring of butterflies on sites is also important, particularly on reserves where one needs to distinguish between natural fluctuations and the effects of various land management operations. A method of monitoring butterflies has been devised by the Institute of Terrestrial Ecology, which is being carried out on a network of individual sites throughout the country. Weekly counts of butterflies are made along a fixed transect from April until September. The transect is chosen to include a representative sample of habitat types within the site and could include areas which are being actively managed. The results show the yearly fluctuations in abundance and if the site is monitored for a number of years, it may be possible to determine whether the management is proving to be beneficial or detrimental to a butterfly population. A booklet explaining the method can be obtained from the Institute of Terrestrial Ecology[25].

Butterfly introductions

To many people the simple approach to butterfly conservation would be to release large numbers of attractive butterflies into the countryside. Such butterflies can easily be bred in quantity in glasshouses. In 1984 a scheme to release various species into a London park was well publicised. The problem with these introductions is that unless the habitat is right in every respect, the released butterflies will die in a day or two without breeding, and criticism of the London scheme eventually caused it to be abandoned. However, the release of butterflies does happen on a much smaller scale. There is a small band of enthusiasts who have developed the considerable expertise necessary to breed almost all of the British butterflies in their back gardens. If successful, high numbers can be produced and surplus stock is often released into the countryside. An introduction may be deliberately attempted onto a site where the species has not previously been recorded. In some cases the butterflies may survive for several years, but in most cases they do not – simply because the habitat is unsuitable in some way. One problem with such illicit introductions is that it becomes impossible to distinguish between a natural extension in range, which does occur from time to time, and an artificial introduction.

There is a place for the use of introductions in butterfly conservation, particularly on nature reserves where a rare species has been lost and where the habitat has since been managed to provide the optimum breeding conditions. However, before attempting such an introduction, the approval and advice of the Nature Conservancy Council should first be sought.

Chequered skipper
Carterocephalus palaemon

The chequered skipper was last recorded in Oxfordshire in the mid-1920s and by 1975 was declared extinct in England, having rapidly disappeared from its strongholds in the east midlands. It is now only found in the west of Scotland in the Lochaber and Argyll districts, where it flies in grassy woodland clearings or along lightly wooded stream valleys. Chequered skippers are usually seen singly or in small groups, and the males appear to be territorial in their behaviour. They can be found basking on grasses or bracken with open wings, or feeding from flowers such as bluebell and bugle.

The butterflies have a dark brown ground colour marked with a pattern of orange-yellow cells. The underside forewing is similar to the upperside except that the cells are longer and the ground colour lighter. The underside hindwing has an olive green ground colour.

Eggs are laid singly on blades of grasses; purple moor-grass is probably widely used in Scotland, while the English colonies were feeding on false-brome and other grasses. The larvae live in tubes of grass constructed by spinning together the edges of the grass blades. The mature larva overwinters in a hibernaculum spun amongst the grass. Pupation takes place in April, the butterfly emerges from early to late May, and remains on the wing for up to one month.

The butterfly occurred formerly at Wychwood Forest, Enstone, Bruern Wood and other un-named localities in Oxfordshire[3], while in Buckinghamshire a certain Rev. C. F. Thornwell reported it from the north border of the county near Whittlebury Forest[12]. The reason for the sad demise of this butterfly can only be guessed at but it seems likely to be due to a number of different factors rather than just habitat loss or change. It is possible that the butterfly still survives in England and is therefore a species worth looking out for, especially in some of the larger and less well known woods.

EXTINCT

Small skipper
Thymelicus sylvestris

Small skippers fly in almost any area of rough grassland where the grass is tall and not closely cropped. Roadside verges, open woodland rides, downland, uncut meadows and urban wasteland are all haunts of this lively butterfly. The butterflies have a short, rapid and buzzing flight. When basking they have a distinctive 'skipper' pose, with the forewings half open and the hindwings fully open and flat. Small skippers feed on nectar from a range of flowers and are particularly fond of thistles, knapweed and red clover. Groups of up to twelve individuals are often seen together at one clump of flowers.

The upperside of the wings is light orange-brown, bordered with a black and white fringe. The veins are black near the margin. The underside of the wings is pale orange with an olive tint on the hindwings. Males have an oblique black stripe on the forewing upperside, which distinguishes them from the females. The antennae are black on the upperside and yellow on the underside; the undersides of the tips are yellowish-orange — not black as in the Essex skipper.

Eggs are laid in batches inside the leaf sheaths of grasses, including Yorkshire-fog and cocksfoot. The minute first instar larvae spin a protective cocoon inside the leaf sheath, where they hibernate for winter. Larvae commence feeding in April and construct protective tubes by binding grass blades together. The final instar larvae are green in colour and emerge from the leaf sheaths for short periods until pupation. The pupa, which is green marked with pink, is protected in a coarse cocoon spun amongst grass stems. The butterflies emerge in early July, about three weeks later than the large skipper, and are on the wing until late August.

The small skipper is found throughout the three counties and may be seen in large numbers in suitable habitats. However, it is rare in heavily grazed pasture and the number of colonies has probably been greatly reduced by the intensification of agriculture in many parts of the three counties.

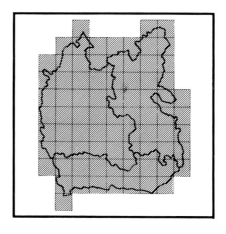

Essex skipper
Thymelicus lineola

Essex skippers fly in very much the same places as small skippers and the two are often seen flying together. However, when together there is usually a preponderence of one species - they are rarely seen in equal numbers.

The Essex skipper has a very similar appearance to the small skipper, with the same orange ground colour. The scent mark on the male upperside is shorter and less oblique than in the small skipper. The best distinguishing feature is the antenna where the Essex skipper has a black tip to the club, as if it had been dipped in a pot of ink. The underside of the antenna tip in the small skipper is yellowish-orange.

The flat eggs are laid inside sheaths of grass such as cocksfoot and creeping soft-grass — dead stems are often chosen. Unlike the small skipper, the eggs do not hatch until the following spring. The larvae spin leaf blades into tubes where they live solitarily. The head capsule of the larva is a distinctive brown and white colour, and quite different from that of the small skipper. The larva pupates in a coarse cocoon which is formed within spun grass leaves. Essex skippers emerge two weeks later than small skippers and fly in July and August.

The Essex skipper was only distinguished from the small skipper in England in 1889, and was first believed to be restricted to wetlands in the south-eastern counties. There are no old records of the butterfly in our region and it was first recorded from Bernwood Forest in 1946. Today Essex skippers are widespread in east Buckinghamshire and east Berkshire where they may be more abundant than small skippers. There are scattered records of Essex skippers throughout our region. However, because of problems of identification it may be under-recorded. It seems reasonable to assume that it is spreading westwards from its stronghold in the east. Perhaps it is colonizing along its favoured roadside verge habitat? It will be interesting to see whether this expansion continues and whether there is any change in the abundance of small skippers.

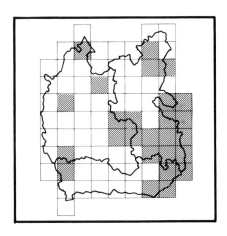

Silver-spotted skipper
Hesperia comma

Silver-spotted skippers are restricted to chalk and limestone hills of southern England, and are particular in their choice of habitat. Steep, south-facing slopes are preferred, and very short turf with abundant sheep's-fescue is a prime requirement. They are only active in warm sunshine and rarely rise much above the ground. The swift, buzzing flight is difficult to follow, but the butterfly will often stop to bask on the ground or feed from a flower — dwarf thistles are a particular favourite.

The uppersides have an orange-brown ground colour with dark brown patterning, and a series of yellow spots near the tip of the wing. The underside is greenish with silvery-white rectangular spots, from which the common name is derived.

The whitish eggs are helmet-shaped and are laid on small clumps of sheep's-fescue. These eggs overwinter and hatch during March and April. The larva spins several grass blades together to form a tent in which it lives for three to four months, emerging only at night to feed upon the surrounding grass. The pupa is protected in a coarse cocoon at the base of the grass stems. The butterfly emerges in early August and flies until early September.

The silver-spotted skipper is one of the region's rarest butterflies — in fact nationally this species has shown a dramatic decline during the past thirty years. In our area the butterfly is restricted to the Chilterns and Berkshire Downs and there are old records from nearly fifteen sites. Today there are only about half a dozen colonies left and five of these are in the Chilterns. Reasons for this decline include the ploughing of downland after 1945, and the reduction in grazing following myxomatosis in the early 1950s.

Although the largest colony is on land owned by the National Trust, and three other colonies are on nature reserves, the silver-spotted skipper remains under threat in our area and its survival will depend on sympathetic management by land owners.

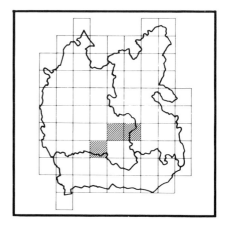

Large skipper
Ochlodes venata

The large skipper will fly in a wide range of places where unimproved grassland is present. It does, however, prefer ungrazed areas of long grass especially where there is some shelter. South-facing downland slopes, woodland rides and clearings, and uncut roadside verges are typical habitats frequented by the large skipper. It is a very active and restless butterfly, constantly alighting on grasses and small shrubs. It will bask in sunshine with its forewings raised and partly open and the hindwings fully open and flat. When feeding on flowers or roosting, its wings are closed over its back.

The upperside of the wings is orange with brown markings and dark brown veins. The males are smaller and less heavily marked than the females, and also possess conspicuous dark scent marks on the forewings. The underside is orange-brown with green shading, and the markings are lighter than on the upperside.

The eggs are laid singly on the blades of grasses such as cocksfoot, false-broome and tor-grass. The newly hatched larvae are primrose yellow with a black head, but later instar larvae are bluish green in colour. The larva constructs a tube by pulling together two blades of grass with strands of silk, to provide shelter between feeding periods. The half grown larvae hibernate in September and recommence feeding in March. The pupa, hidden in a cocoon constructed amongst blades of grass, is situated low down at the base of a grass tussock. The butterfly emerges over a long period and is on the wing from early to mid-June until August. Faded specimens might be confused at a glance with small skippers, but with a little practice none of the British skippers should cause any problems of identification.

These lively butterflies are widespread in our region and almost certainly occur in every 10 km square. The large skipper is a relatively solitary species and is seldom found in the same large numbers as the small skipper. The largest populations are found in open woodland or scrubby downland.

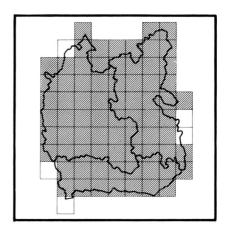

Dingy skipper
Erynnis tages

Dingy skippers occur in a range of habitats such as rough grassland, open woodland, heathland and old quarries, and the largest colonies are found on well-drained chalk and limestone areas. The butterflies are very active in sunshine and have a rapid, buzzing flight, usually keeping close to the ground. They often bask with their wings fully open, but in cool weather and at night they roost on dead flower or grass heads, where they lay their wings along their body to provide perfect camouflage.

This rather moth-like butterfly is small and fuscous brown in colour, marked with darker brown and white. The underside is golden-brown speckled with cream-coloured markings.

The distinctive keeled eggs are laid singly on the base of a leaflet of common bird's-foot trefoil. The egg is yellow when first laid but soon turns bright orange. The larva constructs a tent by spinning a few leaflets together, and emerges at night to feed. In August, when the larva is fully grown, a more substantial cocoon is constructed in which the winter is passed. The larva pupates in the same cocoon the following spring. The butterfly emerges in May and can be seen on the wing until late June. A partial second brood in August has been reported but this only occurs during a particularly hot summer.

Although reasonably widespread in the Chilterns and Berkshire Downs, dingy skippers are never abundant and usually occur in small, discrete colonies where common bird's-foot trefoil is plentiful. Being a rather inconspicuous butterfly, it may be under-recorded. However, their distribution is certainly limited by the shortage of rough, unimproved grassland which they favour. Dingy skippers were formerly much more widespread than now. Reasons for this decline include the increased intensity of farming in the north of our region, the scrubbing over of downland following the cessation of grazing — particularly since the advent of myxomatosis in 1953, and the decline of traditional woodland management leading to the neglect of woodland rides.

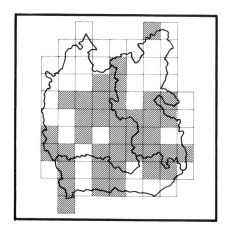

Grizzled skipper
Pyrgus malvae

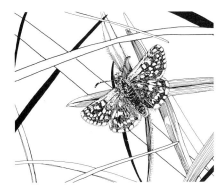

Grizzled skippers are denizens of sheltered, unimproved grasslands. They fly on downland, in sheltered meadows or along dry woodland rides, and are most frequently found where the soils are calcareous. The butterflies often bask with their wings fully open and have a swift, low flight which can be difficult to follow. They sometimes fly with dingy skippers, and both seem in many ways, more like moths than butterflies. At night or in dull conditions, grizzled skippers rest with their wings tightly closed over their backs and the colouring and marking of the hind wings makes them very inconspicuous.

The upperside of this small butterfly is black, patterned with white, giving a very distinctive 'chessboard' effect. The underside of the forewing is patterned like the upperside but the hindwing is brown and white. The sexes are similarly marked and not easy to distinguish, but as in the dingy skipper the males have folds in the forewings which show as tiny white lines.

Eggs are laid singly, usually on the underside of leaves of the foodplant, which can be wild strawberry, tormentil or creeping cinquefoil. First instar larvae live under a web of silk on the upperside of a leaf. After the second moult, they spin entire leaves together and then feed within these tents. The pupa is formed inside a loose cocoon at the base of the foodplant, where it survives the winter. The butterfly is on the wing in May and June. A partial second brood may appear in August in exceptionally warm summers.

Grizzled skippers are not common in our region but there are scattered records throughout the three counties. They are most numerous in the Chilterns, Berkshire Downs and well-wooded areas. It is interesting to note that in several places grizzled skippers are thriving in dry, open rides of conifer plantations. They were more widespread in the early years of this century and it seems reasonable to suggest that their contraction is due in part to the loss of much suitable habitat through agricultural improvement.

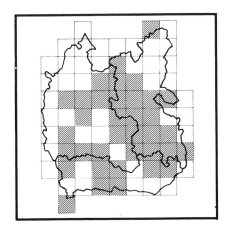

Wood white
Leptidea sinapis

The wood white is essentially a woodland butterfly, and is easily recognized by its weak and very distinctive flight. The upperside of the male is white with dark grey apical patches. The underside is white suffused with grey, and sometimes the whole ground colour is tinged with yellow. Females are similarly marked but their forewings are more rounded and the apical patch tends to be fainter.

Wood whites lay their eggs on a range of legumes including meadow vetchling, bitter vetch and common bird's-foot trefoil. The elongated egg is pale yellow in colour and is laid on the underside of a leaf of its food plant. The green larva rests along the leaf edge and does not move far from the egg site, except prior to pupation. The pupa is secured to a nearby stem by a silken girdle, and is similar in shape to the orange tip pupa. The butterflies emerge in late May and the flight period may extend well into July. In warm summers there may be a small second brood in August.

The wood white is a very local species nationally and the woodland areas of eastern Oxfordshire and north-western Bucking-hamshire are important centres for this species. In 1976 wood whites were seen in many new haunts — probably a response to the abnormally hot summers of 1975 and 1976. Since that time wood whites have expanded their range and each year have been recorded from new places. In 1984, for example, single specimens were seen at two sites in the Chilterns.

A number of colonies have been found along railway embankments, but the usual habitat is woodland rides and clearings, and many colonies are in conifer plantations. Such a plantation however, will only support a colony in the early to middle stages, before the trees mature and shade out the larval food plants. Thus unless adequate conservation measures are taken we may see a decline in the status of this delightful butterfly during the next decade.

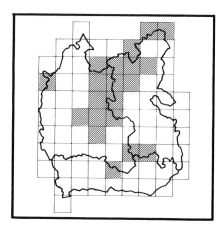

Clouded yellow
Colias croceus

The clouded yellow is one of our scarcer migrant butterflies, its home being the Mediterranean region. The butterflies are catholic in their choice of habitat and may be seen in gardens, along roadside verges, and in herb-rich meadows. They are perhaps most numerous in lucerne and clover fields — these fields providing a food source for the larvae. This beautiful butterfly cannot be confused with any of the other whites and has a distinctive strong, rapid flight. It does not rest with the wings open and only stops briefly to feed on flowers.

Clouded yellows have orange uppersides with black margins to both hind and forewings. The underside is a greenish-yellow with a black spot on the forewing, and a central, reddish-ringed silver spot on the hindwing. Females are larger than males and the upperside dark border has some yellow spots. There is a common female form (*helice*) where the ground colour is white or pale yellow.

The eggs are laid singly on a range of legumes including vetches, lucerne and clover. The larvae feed up quickly and there can be several broods in a season. The yellowish-green pupae can be found attached to the foodplant.

In most years no clouded yellows are seen in our region, and in other years only one or two sightings are made. However, in certain years they occur in abundance. The best post-war 'clouded yellow year' was 1947, but more recently 1983 produced a considerable influx to our region. Butterflies were seen flying northwards near Oxford on June 7, and subsequently there were many sightings from all over the three counties. Breeding was proved at a number of sites but the adults were never seen in groups of more than about six. Fresh individuals were seen as late as October 10, which suggests that there may have been two or even three English broods.

The clouded yellow makes a welcome addition to our butterfly fauna and let us hope that clouded yellow years occur more frequently in future.

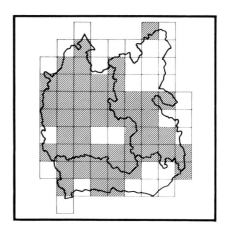

Brimstone
Gonepteryx rhamni

The brimstone is a familiar and welcome butterfly of early spring. On the first warm days in February and March, this butterfly emerges from hibernation and may be seen winging its way along lanes, hedgerows, gardens and woodland rides. The yellow males are first on the wing and are more often noticed than the paler females.

The upperside of the male is a bright sulphur yellow with reddish spots at the end of the veins and a single spot in the centre of each wing. The underside is duller in colour and the spots are brown. The females are similarly marked but the ground colour is a light whitish-green. The shape and colouring of the wings is very leaf like and when at rest amongst vegetation, the butterflies are well camouflaged. A mating pair has even been seen resting in the corolla tube of a wild daffodil, providing an example of perfect camouflage.

Eggs are laid on two species of buckthorn; buckthorn and alder buckthorn, although in our area the former species is commoner and more widely used. The cigar-shaped eggs are easily found in May or June and are laid on the undersides of the leaves, usually towards the terminal shoots. The green larvae rest along the mid-ribs of the leaves and their cryptic colouration make them difficult to find. The larvae usually pupate away from buckthorn.

The males and females emerge together in July and do not pair, but spend the rest of the summer feeding up before hibernation. They feed avidly on a range of flowers, including thistles, teasel, marjoram and even runner bean flowers, and will often visit the same patch of flowers day after day. Brimstones may be seen flying as late as October until they all retire to hibernation.

The distribution map clearly shows brimstones to be widespread and it is probable that they occur in every 10 km square. These butterflies are strong fliers and are often seen well away from known buckthorn bushes.

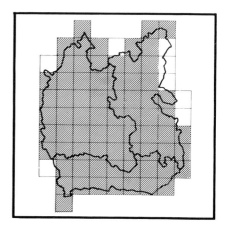

Large white
Pieris brassicae

Large whites may be seen in almost any habitat but are most common in the vicinity of habitation — allotment gardens are particularly favoured because of the abundance of cultivated *brassicas* which are the food plants of the larvae. The large white, and its close relative the small white, are often called 'cabbage whites' and are the only butterfly species in this country which cause damage to crops. The butterflies are often seen taking nectar from a range of flowers including dandelions, hawkbits and garden flowers such as buddleia. They fly strongly and will range widely into the surrounding countryside.

The upperside is predominantly white with black markings. Males have black tips to the forewing and a black spot on the front margin of the hindwing. Females have two black spots and a black dash on the forewing, in addition to the markings shown by the males. Both sexes have hindwing undersides dusted with yellow-green, which provide a degree of camouflage when the butterflies are at rest.

The yellow eggs are laid in batches on a suitable food plant. Apart from garden *brassicas*, it is possible that several wild crucifers are used. The small larvae are gregarious and possess an unpleasant smell which may be a defence against predators. The final instar larvae have a grey ground colour with yellow and black markings, and may be found wandering away from the food plant searching for a suitable pupation site. A tree trunk or wall is often chosen and the pupa has a similar colouration to that of the larva.

The large white normally has two generations a year and the first brood may be seen from the end of April in mild seasons until late June, and the second brood from late July to September. Overwintering takes place in the pupal stage. Numbers vary considerably from year to year and are often boosted by migratory butterflies from the continent. Occasionally the butterfly is very scarce, usually after a heavy infestation of the parasitic wasp, *Apanteles glomeratus*, which destroys the larvae.

Large whites are widespread and abundant in the three counties.

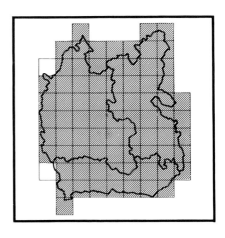

Small white
Pieris rapae

The small white is a familiar butterfly in our gardens and allotments, especially near the cabbage patch where it causes a small amount of damage. They are also seen throughout the countryside, where they are attracted to nectar plants such as thistles, knapweeds and dandelions. In spite of being considered a pest by gardeners, small whites are delicate butterflies which are particularly attractive when sunshine is seen filtering through their translucent wings.

Small whites have a white upper surface with black markings. Males have a black tip to each forewing and a single black spot. Females have an additional black spot, a dash on the forewing, and are usually yellower in colour. In the spring brood these markings tend to be grey whereas in the summer brood the markings are darker and more pronounced. The undersides of both male and female are similar — the forewing has a yellow tip and two black spots, and the hindwing is dusted with yellow.

Eggs are laid singly on the underside of the food plant's leaves — garden *brassicas* are favoured but nasturtiums and wild crucifers such as garlic mustard and hedge mustard are also selected. The green larvae are solitary and often found in the heart of younger leaves of *brassicas*. They rest along a midrib or vein of a leaf, where they are extremely well camouflaged. Small white larvae wander off the food plant to find a pupation site and in so doing are often taken by birds. They pupate on tree trunks, fences or buildings and the pupae are variable in colour with green and brown being common forms; this colour is determined by the background colour of the pupation site.

The pupae of the second brood overwinter and the butterflies emerge in the spring during early April, and may be seen until September. The second generation is much larger than the first and it is likely that numbers are reinforced by immigrants. In favourable seasons there may be a partial third brood in September.

Small whites are widespread and abundant in the three counties and occur in every 10 km square.

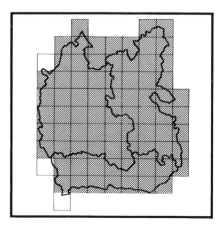

Green-veined white
Pieris napi

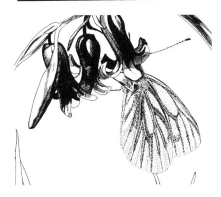

Green-veined whites are butterflies of the countryside and, unlike the two 'cabbage whites', are not frequently seen near habitation. Woodland rides, sheltered lanes and damp meadows are typical habitats. They are attractive butterflies and may be seen in large groups of up to fifty individuals, where there are concentrations of nectar and larval host plants.

The ground colour of the upperside is usually white, although variation does occur, occasionally producing a yellow colouration. The male has a black apex to the forewing, a black spot and some darkening along the veins. Females have an extra black spot, a black dash on the forewing and in general they are more heavily marked. The sexes have similar undersides with black spots on the forewing and a yellow apex, and a yellow ground colour to the hindwing. The veins are outlined in black giving an illusion of green, which gives rise to the butterfly's common name and distinguishes it from the small white.

The eggs are laid singly on a range of wild crucifers such as cuckoo flower and garlic mustard — cultivated *brassicas* are not used and so this species is not a garden pest. The cryptically coloured larva feeds on the leaves of the food plant, unlike the orange tip which shares the same plants but feeds on the developing seed pods. The larva pupates away from the food plant, and the pupa may vary in colour from green to light brown, depending on the colour of the background. Green-veined whites overwinter as pupae and can be seen on the wing in April. They are double-brooded and the early generation is over by mid-June. The summer brood is on the wing in July and August and occasionally there is a small third brood.

The green-veined white is widespread and common in our area and is likely to occur in every 10 km square. This species may be confused with the small white, but a study of its habits and flight characteristics will soon enable the observer to distinguish these two butterflies.

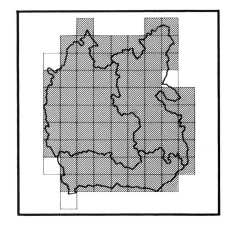

Orange tip
Anthocharis cardamines

This delightful spring butterfly occurs in a range of different habitats wherever a combination of larval food plants, nectar and shelter are found. Quiet country lanes, woodland ride and edge, river banks and wet unimproved meadows are all likely haunts. The butterflies are very active and males will spend long periods searching for females. They will stop to feed from flowers such as ragged-robin and bugle, but only for a few seconds — photographers know orange tips as elusive subjects.

The upperside of the male is white with bright orange apical patches on the forewings. On the underside the orange is more sub-dued, and the whole of the hind-wing is covered with mottled greenish-yellow and white col-ouration. The females differ in that the tips of the wings are dap-pled with black and grey. At a glance females could be confused with small and green-veined whites, but the green mottled underside is distinctive. Orange tips frequently rest on flower heads of cow parsley where the patterned undersides provide marvellous camouflage.

Eggs are laid singly in the young flower heads of garlic mustard, cuckoo flower and other cruciferous plants. The elongated eggs are off-white when first laid but later change to a bright orange. The young larvae feed on the developing seed pods and when at rest are well camouflaged. They usually leave the food plant to pupate and the pupae can be either green or brown. Overwinter-ing takes place in the pupal stage. The butterflies emerge in early May and are on the wing for four to six weeks.

Orange tips are widespread in our area, but are rarely abundant. The loss of damp meadows and widespread hedge removal during the post-war period of intensive farming undoubtedly destroyed a large number of colonies. In recent years the species has also suffered from excessive cutting of roadside verges, although present cut backs of local authority spen-ding seem to have reduced this activity, and we may hope to see more orange tips patrolling our lanes in future.

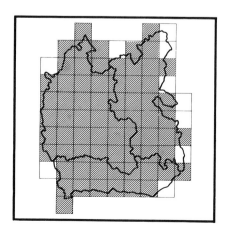

Green hairstreak
Callophrys rubi

The green hairstreak may be found in a variety of habitats, but prefers rough ground where there are plenty of shrubs. Typical haunts are scrubby downland, heathland, woodland glades and rides, and railway embankments. This exquisite little butterfly is amusing to watch. The males are territorial and will perch for much of the day on prominent shrubs such as hawthorn and gorse. They make periodic short flights to investigate passing butterflies and usually return back to the same perch. Green hairstreaks have been seen taking nectar from common rock-rose, common bird's-foot trefoil and wood spurge. It is possible that, like other hairstreaks, they also feed on a sticky, sweet aphid-secretion called honeydew.

As the only green British butterfly, green hairstreaks are quite unmistakable. Only the underside however, is green and when at rest with closed wings, the butterfly is very inconspicuous. There are also brown scales on the underside which are particularly evident in older individuals when some green scales have been lost. The uppersides of the wings are brown but these are only ever glimpsed on the butterfly in flight.

Pale green eggs are laid singly on young shoots or in the flower buds of a wide variety of plants including common rock-rose, dyer's greenweed, gorse and dogwood. The green and yellow striped larvae, which are well camouflaged and feed by day, have the typical 'woodlouse-shape' of all hairstreaks. The pupae overwinter in leaf litter near the food plant and are said to have the capacity to squeak if disturbed. The butterflies emerge over a long period and are on the wing in May, June and July.

Green hairstreaks are thinly spread in our area and their stronghold is in the Chilterns. In the Berkshire Downs they only survive near the few remaining areas of scrub. On acid soils in Berkshire they often occur at the shrubby edges of woodland, rather than on the more exposed areas of heathland. In the clay vales green hairstreaks are rare except near areas of ancient woodland.

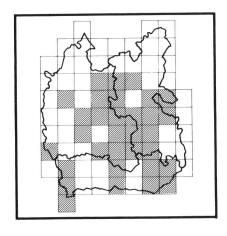

Brown hairstreak
Thecla betulae

The brown hairstreak is a scarce butterfly in Britain and is chiefly found in well-wooded areas where there are plenty of blackthorn thickets and hedges. The butterflies are rather elusive and spend much of their time at the tops of bushes and trees. Here they congregate for mating and also to feed on honeydew. Occasionally they will come down to feed on nectar, and favourite flowers are brambles, thistles and ragwort. The females are more readily seen than the males, particularly when they are egg-laying. They can be found in blackthorn hedges, crawling along the twigs searching for a suitable place to deposit an egg. Between egg-laying periods, they often bask in the sunshine with open wings.

The upperside of the female is a deep chocolate brown with a large orange patch on the forewing, and three orange marks on each hindwing. The male uppersides differ in that the orange markings are smaller and paler. The undersides, which are similar in both sexes, have a beautiful golden-brown colour which is marked with black lines and white stripes, and a reddish marginal band.

The white eggs are particularly conspicuous during the winter months when the blackthorn twigs are bare. Smaller bushes are usually chosen, often in hedges adjoining woods. The larvae hatch in early May and their pale green colouration marked with light yellow enables them to be perfectly camouflaged against a blackthorn leaf. The brown pupa can be found in leaf litter under the blackthorn bush. In early August the butterflies emerge and are on the wing until late September.

Brown hairstreaks are rare in the three counties and have their stronghold on the clays around Oxford. They have been recorded in the Chilterns and there are old and unconfirmed records from Berkshire, but the elusiveness of the butterfly does mean that it may be under-recorded. Threats to its survival include the loss of hedgerows, and the increasing intensity of hedge management, whereby annual winter trimming can remove a high percentage of brown hairstreak eggs.

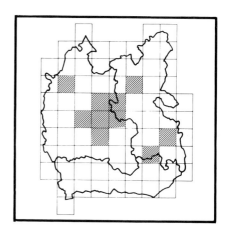

Purple hairstreak
Quercusia quercus

The purple hairstreak is a common woodland butterfly which probably occurs in every oak-dominated wood in the three counties. The butterflies spend much of their time near the tops of oak and ash trees, feeding on honeydew. Once recognized, the flight of purple hairstreaks up in these trees is unmistakable — a glint of the silvery grey underside is usually seen. In some years they are seen in great numbers and will continue flying until dusk. They are early risers and will sometimes come down to bask on lower branches to catch the morning sun. In very dry years such as 1976 purple hairstreaks were seen probing for moisture on bare ground.

The male uppersides are a dark purplish-blue with a black border. The purple colour is iridescent and only shows at certain angles of vision. The females have a much smaller area of purplish-blue on the forewings. The underside of both sexes is grey marked with brown and white lines. There are two orange spots, one of which is black-centred, on the hindwing.

The greyish eggs are laid on oak twigs near to the buds, and are easy to find during winter. The larvae hatch in spring, and feed within expanding buds. The later instar larvae which are light brown patterned with dark brown, closely resemble bud scales. Pupation usually occurs on the ground under leaf litter or moss. The butterflies emerge in mid-July and are on the wing until late August.

Purple hairstreaks are widely distributed in the three counties but because of their elusiveness are almost certainly under-recorded. However, careful study of many oak woods in 1984, revealed that the hairstreaks were always present. Past records suggest that the purple hairstreak was more widespread during the early years of this century, before large scale fellings of oak woodland during the two world wars. Many of these oak woods have been converted to conifer plantations which must have greatly reduced the numbers of this charming butterfly.

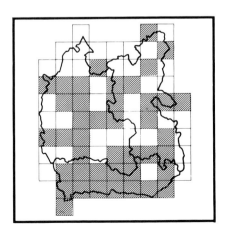

White-letter hairstreak
Strymonidia w-album

White-letter hairstreaks fly in the vicinity of elms; in open deciduous woodland, at woodland edges and in sheltered, mature hedgerows. They spend much of their time amongst the foliage of elm and other trees and it may be necessary to use binoculars to confirm identification. Although honeydew is their preferred food source, the butterflies do occasionally come down to feed on nectar; brambles, wild privet and thistles are the most favoured flowers.

The upperside of both sexes is dark brown, although this will only be glimpsed in flight as the butterfly always settles with its wings closed. The underside is brown with a thin white line running across both wings and forming a 'W' towards the bottom angle of the hindwing. The hindwing also has a band of black and orange markings near the margin.

The flattened 'flying-saucer shape' egg is laid on the underside of elm twigs, usually near the junction between last year's and the present year's growth. Eggs survive the winter and hatch towards the end of February. The larvae feed in the opening flower buds and then move on to the seeds and leaves. The dark brown pupae are found on the undersides of leaves, often lying adjacent to the mid-rib. The butterflies emerge in mid-July and the flight season lasts for about a month.

Prior to Dutch elm disease, white-letter hairstreaks were widespread in our region and were even found on elms in urban areas. However, populations were known to fluctuate tremendously from year to year, and in the early years of this century it was said to be *a very uncertain species, abounding in one season, scarce for many successive years'* in Buckinghamshire[2]. During the period 1975-83 almost all the mature elms were killed in the three counties and several colonies are known to have become extinct. Naturally there was concern that this attractive butterfly would be lost[13]. However, by 1984 it became clear that several colonies had survived, some of which appear to be existing on non-flowering saplings and sucker growth from diseased elms.

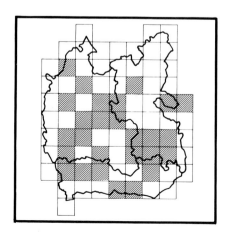

Black hairstreak
Strymonidia pruni

The black hairstreak is a rare woodland butterfly confined to the low-lying basin between Oxford and Peterborough. It occurs in woods with substantial blackthorn thickets, often along a sheltered woodland edge or in sunny rides and clearings. The adults are elusive and spend much of their time amongst the upper branches of blackthorn and neighbouring trees. However, when they are newly emerged they often come down to perch on low herbage and this is a good time to observe them. Although they usually feed on honeydew, in some years they visit flowers and have been seen taking nectar from bramble, wild privet and hogweed.

The upperside of the female is dark brown with orange marks near the wing borders. In the male the orange marks are only on the hindwing. The underside of both sexes is a golden-brown with a thin white line across both wings. There is a row of black dots on the inside of the orange borders to the hindwings.

The eggs are laid singly on blackthorn, usually on the bark of one to three year old growth, and do not hatch until the following spring. The larvae feed on the opening buds and later on the leaves. The pupa is spun on a leaf or stem and looks remarkably like a bird dropping. The butterflies emerge in late June and fly for about three weeks.

In our region black hairstreaks can only be found in parts of Oxfordshire and north Buckinghamshire, and since 1975 have been recorded from ten 10 km squares. Most of the colonies are on the heavy Oxford clay and many have persisted for over a hundred years. An intensive study during the early 1970s identified 25 recorded colonies. A field survey (1970-73) provided evidence of breeding at only 16 of these sites, and five of the colonies had almost certainly become extinct because the wood had either been clear felled or coniferised[14]. Since 1975 the butterfly has been discovered at three new sites, two of which are to the south and west of the previous known range.

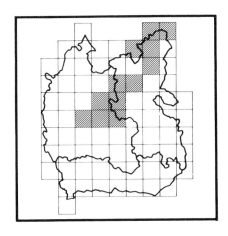

Small copper
Lycaena phlaeas

Small coppers occur in a variety of habitats from downland to heathland, rough grassland and waste ground. Indeed any area of unimproved grassland with sorrels or docks, the larval foodplants, may support a colony of this delightful butterfly. Small coppers often fly with common blues and they can be seen feeding together on plants such as ragwort and common fleabane.

On the upperside, the ground colour of the forewing is a brilliant coppery-orange, marked with black spots. These wings are edged by a black border and white fringe. The hindwing is dark brown with a wavy orange band near the white fringe. On the underside the forewing is pale orange spotted with black, and the hindwing is light brown with a thin red band near the border. The flashes of orange as these butterflies fly swiftly from flower to flower are unmistakable.

The distinctive golf-ball shaped eggs are laid on a number of different species of *Rumex* although common sorrel and sheep's sorrel are most widely used. The young larvae perforate the leaves in a characteristic manner, thus enabling easy detection. Mature larvae can be either green or green striped with pink. The latter form is rarer but both forms provide excellent camouflage on the foodplants. Half-grown larvae of the third brood hibernate on a pad of silk on the underside of a leaf and resume feeding in the spring. Pupation takes place on the plant or nearby in low vegetation, and the first brood is on the wing in May and June. The second brood emerges in July and August, and in some years there is a third brood, with individuals flying as late as the end of October.

The small copper is widespread in our area. Colonies tend to be small and the butterflies are rarely seen in groups of more than two or three. The second brood is always more numerous than the first and so August is the best month for seeing this attractive little butterfly.

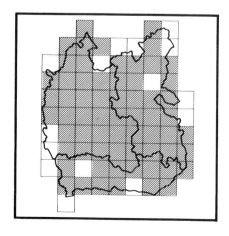

Small blue
Cupido minimus

The small blue is confined to chalk and limestone areas where kidney vetch, its larval foodplant, grows. The butterfly has a particular requirement for warm, sheltered situations and is found in quarries, railway cuttings and on south-facing downland slopes. They often fly just above the ground and may be found basking on broad-leaved grasses with out-spread wings.

As their name suggests, the butterflies are very small and rather inconspicuous. The males have a sooty black upperside with a dusting of blue scales. The females are browner in colour and lack any blue coloration. The underside of both sexes is pale grey with a number of tiny, white-ringed black dots. The underside could be confused at a glance with the holly blue, but the smaller size and dark upperside should avoid any difficulties of identification.

The small eggs, laid singly amongst the flowers of a kidney vetch inflorescence, are easy to find. The young larvae bore into the flower heads and feed on developing seeds. When fully mature, the larvae leave the seed heads to hibernate on the ground.

Pupation takes place the following May, and the butterflies emerge at the beginning of June. They are on the wing for about a month and in many summers a partial second brood may be seen in August.

The small blue is very local in the calcareous areas of the three counties. The colonies are frequently small and tend to breed year after year in the same discrete sites. The stronghold of the small blue is in the Chilterns, although a number of colonies have been lost on sites which have become overgrown following the decline in rabbit and sheep grazing. There are small scattered colonies on the Berkshire Downs, where most are restricted to banks and edges of trackways across the Downs. Several colonies also occur on the oolitic limestone of north and west Oxfordshire, and there is a particularly large colony at an actively worked quarry near Banbury.

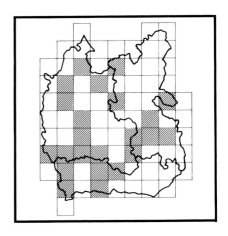

Silver-studded blue
Plebejus argus

The silver-studded blue is one of our few true heathland butterflies and is locally common on some of the larger acid heathlands in southern England. The butterflies fly low over vegetation and are often seen in groups basking or resting on heather and gorse bushes. They will also feed on nectar from heather flowers.

The upperside of the male is mauve-blue with black borders and white fringes. The ground colour of the underside is blue and grey marked with white-ringed black spots. On the hindwing there is a marginal orange band which is marked on the inside with black crescents and on the outside with black spots centred with silvery-blue, which give rise to its common name. The female's upperside is brown with wavy orange marginal bands. At a glance the silver-studded blue could be confused with the common blue, but the combination of the black borders to the wings of the male, the silver studs on the underside, and the heathland habitat should be diagnostic.

The eggs are laid on the woody parts of heather or gorse, the main larval foodplants, or on nearby dead leaves and grass. The mature larvae are green, with a longitudinal black dorsal stripe bordered on each side by a white stripe, and are tended by ants. The pupa is usually formed on the ground near the foodplant, although pupae have also been found inside ant nests. The butterflies emerge in late June and can be seen on the wing until mid-August.

In our region the butterfly is confined to the heathlands of mid and south Berkshire. The larger areas of heathland such as Silchester Common and the patches near Crowthorne support the best colonies. Heathland is a threatened habitat in Berkshire, both through lack of management leading to encroachment by scrub, and through development for housing, agriculture or forestry. There are old records for the Chilterns[12], but as with most other colonies on English chalk and limestone, they are believed to be extinct.

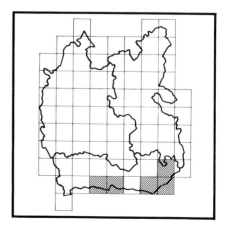

Brown argus
Aricia agestis

The brown argus favours open grassland and is commonest on calcareous soils where common rock-rose, its larval foodplant, grows in profusion. It occurs much less frequently on sandy or clay soils where it uses other foodplants such as dove's-foot cranes-bill. The brown argus is active in bright sunshine and will fly rapidly from flower to flower, often basking with outspread wings. During dull weather and at night they rest, sometimes communally, on the flower-heads and stems of grasses.

The butterflies are small with dark brown uppersides and a row of orange lunules near the white-fringed wing margins. In the female these orange lunules extend right to the apex of the forewing. The underside of the wings, which is greyish-brown in the male and brown in the female, is marked with white-ringed black spots and a submarginal band of orange spots. They are easily confused with female common blues. However, the brown argus tends to be smaller, darker and never has any blue colouration — a combination of characters which usually helps to distinguish the two species.

Eggs are laid singly on the undersides of leaves of the larval foodplant and young larvae feed only on the lower leaf surface, producing characteristic feeding damage similar to that of leaf hoppers. Older larvae eat whole leaves and are usually tended by ants. Half grown larvae of the second brood hibernate and recommence feeding the following spring. Pupation occurs in the turf at the base of the foodplant and the butterflies emerge in early June. The second brood are on the wing in late July and will continue flying until September.

In the three counties the brown argus is locally common in the Chilterns and Berkshire Downs, although a number of colonies have been lost because of the intensification of agriculture, or because of the loss of common rock-rose on ungrazed sites. Away from chalk, small colonies occur on Oxfordshire's corallian and oolitic limestones, and ironstones; and on the acid gravels of west Berkshire.

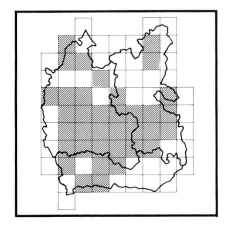

Common blue
Polyommatus icarus

Common blues occur in a variety of habitats including downland, flower-rich meadows, open woodland rides and waste ground — indeed any sunny, grassy area where its larval foodplant, common bird's-foot trefoil grows. The butterflies have a characteristic low and somewhat jerky flight and are very active in sunshine. They are often seen flying with other related species such as small copper and brown argus. They frequently take nectar from flowers such as common fleabane, ragwort and marjoram. In dull weather and at night the butterflies can be found roosting communally on tall grasses.

The male common blue has a mauve-blue upperside with a thin black border and white fringes. The ground colour of the underside is greyish marked with white-ringed black spots and a row of orange lunules towards the wing margins. The female is quite different having a brown upperside with a variable suffusion of blue scales, and a series of orange crescents with black spots near the wing margins. The underside markings are similar to those of the male but the ground colour is brown.

The eggs are laid singly on common bird's-foot trefoil and other leguminous plants such as common restharrow and black medick. The green, hairy larvae feed on the leaves and flowers, and in the final instar possess an active honey gland which is often attended by ants. Larvae of the second brood hibernate in the third instar and resume feeding the following spring. Pupation usually takes place on the ground near the foodplant and the first brood appears on the wing from May to July. The second brood, usually more numerous than the first, can be seen in August and September.

The common blue is the most widespread of our blue butterflies and is likely to occur in every 10 km square. They are found in all but the most intensively farmed parts of our area and will survive on roadside verges. They even breed in garden lawns if common bird's-foot trefoil occurs and the cutting is not too severe.

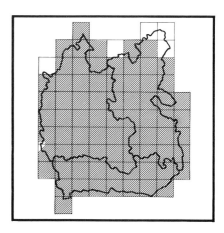

Chalkhill blue
Lysandra coridon

Chalkhill blues, as their name suggests, are confined to calcareous soils because their larval foodplant, horseshoe vetch, only grows on chalk or limestone. The best colonies provide a sensational display of colour, with myriads of silvery-blue butterflies in constant motion.

It is only the male which has the pale silvery-blue upperside with dark borders at the outer margin of the forewings. The female is brown with a row of small orange crescents and black spots around the border of the hindwings, and a row of paler orange marks at the edge of the forewings.

The eggs are laid singly on or near a horseshoe vetch plant, where they survive the winter before hatching the following spring. The larvae feed in the evening and at night and are very attractive to ants which feed on the sweet secretions exuded by the honey gland. The pupa is formed beneath the foodplant on the ground. The butterflies emerge in mid-July. By August they are looking worn but a few survive until early September.

This splendid butterfly can be found in small colonies on the Chilterns and Berkshire Downs. A single colony exists on oolitic limestone in west Oxfordshire, but many of the other records refer to butterflies which have strayed well away from their normal breeding sites. In Bernwood Forest, for example, chalkhill blues have been recorded almost every year since 1976, although the nearest breeding colony is over 10 km away.

This beautiful butterfly has dramatically declined in our area. A number of Berkshire Downs colonies were destroyed by ploughing of their habitat in the 1950s and '60s. A small colony on corallian limestone adjoining Bayswater Brook, within 3 miles of the centre of Oxford, disappeared after most of the site was ploughed in the 1950s. A number of colonies in the Chilterns have been lost from sites which have become overgrown following the cessation of rabbit grazing after myxomatosis. Further declines will occur unless active conservation measures are taken to protect existing areas of downland.

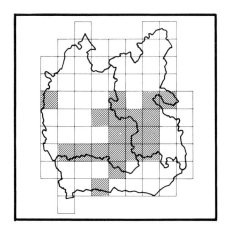

Adonis blue
Lysandra bellargus

The adonis blue is a rare butterfly in southern England and is restricted to calcareous grassland. It is much scarcer and more localised than the chalkhill blue, although they share the same larval foodplant. Its habitat requirements are more precise and it requires warmer conditions. South-facing slopes are preferred and the downland needs to be well-grazed, with a short, fine-leaved sward containing abundant horseshoe vetch.

The male adonis blue is a brilliant iridescent turquoise-blue, and when freshly emerged cannot be confused with any of the other blues. The wing fringes are white with the vein ends showing in black. By contrast the female has a dark brown upperside with a dusting of blue scales near the bases of the wings.

The eggs are laid singly on leaves of horseshoe vetch, usually on plants in sheltered sunspots, where the surrounding vegetation is sparse. Half grown larvae of the second brood hibernate on mats of silk amongst low vegetation, before commencing feeding the following spring. The pupa is protected in a loose cocoon under moss or vegetation, or just below the soil surface. The first brood is on the wing in May and June. The second brood emerges in August and can be seen until mid-September.

The very precise habitat requirements of this butterfly explain its great rarity in our region. Most of the Chiltern slopes are north-facing and the majority are not grazed hard enough to produce the short sward that is so vital to the survival of the species. A number of Chiltern colonies, such as that at Whiteleaf Hill, became extinct in the 1950s and early '60s, when grazing was relaxed after the rabbits had been decimated by myxomatosis[8]. In the Berkshire Downs the adonis blue is very scarce and the remaining colonies are almost too small to be considered as viable populations.

During the period 1980-84 there was one strong and four small adonis blue colonies in the three counties, and so sympathetic management is urgently required if the butterfly is to remain.

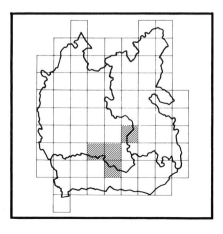

Holly blue
Celastrina argiolus

Unlike the other blues, the holly blue is not an open grassland or heathland butterfly. It is frequently glimpsed, as it flies alongside hedges or settles on leaves, but it does not often pose and rarely takes nectar from flowers. In dry weather it will come down to the ground to seek moisture. It is found in woodland rides, along hedgerows and is often seen in gardens, parks and churchyards, where its larvae feed on a variety of shrubs, including snowberry, *Escallonia* and cultivated varieties of holly and ivy.

The upperside of the male is an azure blue with a lilac tint. The wings are edged with a thin black border and a white fringe. The female is similar in colour but has a broad black border on both fore and hindwings. The underside of both sexes is a pale silvery blue patterned with tiny black spots.

Butterflies of the spring brood lay their eggs on holly and other shrubs such as dogwood and buckthorn. The second brood uses ivy as very few other shrubs are in bud at this time of year. The green, slug-like larvae feed on flower buds and are difficult to see. The pupa is attached to a silk pad on a leaf or twig, and pupae of the second brood overwinter in this stage. The butterflies emerge during April and are on the wing until early June. The second brood flies in July and August.

Holly blues are widespread in the three counties although there is a marked gap in north and east Buckinghamshire. The populations undergo distinct cycles and periodic crashes in numbers are believed to be connected with cycles in abundance of parasitic wasps. At one well recorded site near Oxford, holly blues were not seen for four years between 1980 and 1983, but were recorded again in 1984. Because our recording period included a population crash, it may be that the map understates the true distribution of holly blues. However, this is a familiar species to many people because of its habit of breeding in gardens in many parts of the three counties.

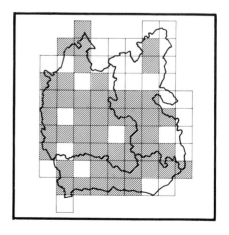

Duke of Burgundy
Hamearis lucina

The Duke of Burgundy occurs on sheltered chalk and limestone grassland, usually in scrubby areas where cowslips are abundant. Less commonly they may occur in open woodland where primroses are selected as the foodplant. These small butterflies fly quickly and are difficult to follow. However, the males are very territorial and will spend much of the day perching on tall grasses, flowers or shrubs. On downland the males congregate in sunny glades among open scrub, whereas in a wood the territories are often established at ride intersections. The males wait on their perches for the females to fly past, and take frequent short flights to inspect any passing butterflies.

The only European member of the predominantly American 'metalmark' family, the Duke of Burgundy has a chequered brown and orange upper surface. The underside of the forewing is similar to the upperside, but the hindwing is brownish with large white cells and black dots near the margin.

The conspicuous, cream coloured eggs are laid in small batches on the undersides of cowslip or primrose leaves. Large, flowering plants are usually chosen, particularly those which are growing in slightly shaded situations. The hairy larvae feed at night on the underside of the leaves, producing characteristic perforations. The pupae survive the winter, hatching in mid-May. The flight season lasts for about five weeks with peak numbers occurring during the last week of May.

The Duke of Burgundy is very local in our region with several small colonies occurring in the Chilterns and Berkshire Downs, and isolated colonies in Oxfordshire, two of which are in limestone quarries. In the Chilterns the Duke of Burgundy is probably nearly as widespread as it was 50 years ago. However, colonies have almost certainly decreased in size and on a number of sites, encroaching scrub is threatening their long term survival. Woodland colonies have now nearly all disappeared following changes in traditional woodland practices leading to the loss of primroses.

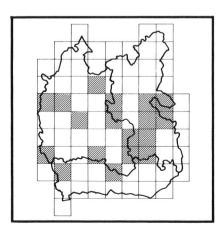

White admiral
Ladoga camilla

The white admiral is confined to woods in southern England, which contain honeysuckle, its larval foodplant. They can be seen flying along rides and glades, often keeping to the edges, and are particularly attracted to bramble bushes, their favourite source of nectar. The females fly into the more shady areas of the wood to search for suitable honeysuckle plants for egg laying.

The upperside is dark brown — almost black, with white bands across all four wings. The underside is a tawny orange with a double row of black spots outside the white band. The basal area of the hind wing is a pearly, blue-grey, which is separated from the white band by an irregular tawny bar. White admirals can be confused with female purple emperors but the smaller size and lack of eye spots on the upperside are distinguishing features.

The eggs are laid singly towards the edge of the upper surface of a honeysuckle leaf. Larvae feed from the leaf tip, on either side of the mid-rib, and this characteristic feeding damage is very easy to find in late summer.

After the second moult, larvae overwinter in a hibernaculum, produced by securing a leaf to the stem with silk, and drawing the edges together to form a tent. Feeding recommences in spring, and in June the larvae pupate on a leaf or stem of the foodplant. The butterflies emerge in early July and are on the wing until mid-August.

White admirals are reasonably widespread in our region and occur in most of the larger woods where conditions are suitable. Although ancient, deciduous woods are perhaps the most typical, coniferous and mixed plantations can also be colonised if honeysuckle is present. Fifty years ago the white admiral was a scarce butterfly. The expansion since the 1930s is said to be the result of a series of favourable seasons when the weather permitted successful breeding[5]. This spread was possibly accelerated by the warm summers of 1975 and 1976 when the butterfly was seen in large numbers all over the three counties.

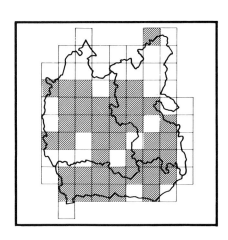

Purple emperor
Apatura iris

The purple emperor is a butterfly confined to the larger tracts of woodland of southern England. It is one of the largest and most handsome of all our butterflies. The adults spend much of their time flying high among the tree canopy and therefore may escape notice. However, the males will often descend to the woodland ride surface, especially during the first week after emergence, to feed on animal droppings, carrion and even the ride surface itself. Recent research has suggested that the butterfly is obtaining salts which are necessary for the reproductive process[15].

The uppersides are dark brown with white spots and bars, and an orange eye spot at the anal angle of the hindwing. In the male the upperside is shot with iridescent purple which changes with the angle of vision. The female, which is slightly larger than the male, completely lacks this purple sheen. The undersides, similar in both sexes, are beautifully marked with a complicated pattern of grey, chestnut, black and white.

Eggs are laid singly on the upper surface of goat willow leaves. The larvae overwinter in the third instar and their colour changes to match the surface on which they are resting. Feeding recommences in spring and mature larvae are superbly camouflaged on the willow leaves. The green pupa is suspended from a leaf and is also very leaf-like. The butterflies emerge in July, usually after the second week, and will fly until mid-August.

Purple emperors are very local in the three counties and are perhaps best represented in the well-wooded parts of south Berkshire, particularly near the Hampshire border. In addition there are several colonies in the ancient woodlands along the Buckinghamshire/Oxfordshire border, and individuals have been sighted at Salcey Forest where it was believed extinct. It has certainly disappeared from a number of woods in north and west Buckinghamshire, and its present status must be considered threatened by the continued loss of deciduous woodland and the loss of breeding habitat in maturing conifer plantations.

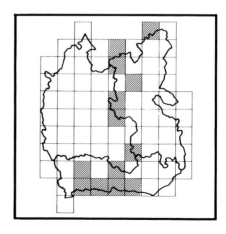

Red admiral
Vanessa atalanta

The red admiral is one of the most familiar of all our butterflies, because of its conspicuous appearance and habit of visiting gardens in almost every part of England. It will also be seen in other habitats such as open woodland, downland and lowland meadows, where there is a combination of shelter, flowers for nectar and larval foodplants. The butterflies are strong fliers and are difficult to follow on the wing. They are fond of feeding on garden flowers including buddleia, ice plant and Michaelmas daisies, and in the autumn are attracted to rotten fruit such as apples and plums. The colour illustration shows a red admiral feeding on ripe berries of wayfaring-tree, and they have been seen feeding in groups on exuding tree sap.

Eggs are laid singly on the terminal leaves of common nettle, usually on plants growing in sunny situations. Each larva spins a leaf to form a tent, in which it feeds. The spiny larvae occur in several different colour forms with dark brown, light brown and olive green being examples. The pupa, which is greyish marked with gold, is also formed within spun leaves.

The butterflies emerge in August and can be seen until mid-October. Most are the progeny of immigrants from the Mediterranean and North Africa which arrive on our shores in early summer. Occasionally butterflies are seen in February and March, and these are thought to be the survivors of those which enter into hibernation in the autumn. In general these splendid butterflies do not survive our cold winters and there is some evidence of a return migration southwards in the autumn.

In the three counties the red admiral is widespread, although numbers will vary greatly from year to year. Numbers have been low over the past four years in our region and it was interesting to note that in 1983, when large numbers of clouded yellow migrants were seen, the red admiral did not appear in such profusion.

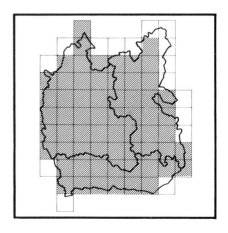

Painted lady
Cynthia cardui

The painted lady is a summer visitor to Britain, arriving from the Mediterranean countries and North Africa. The butterflies are regular visitors to gardens but may be seen in almost any habitat. They are avid nectar feeders and are particularly fond of buddleia flowers. The painted lady is a strong flier but will often return to the same spot day after day. Males are very territorial and will soon chase off other males which enter their territory.

Painted ladies are quite unmistakable because of their large size and distinctive patterning. The ground colour of the upperside can vary from a pale orange to salmon pink. There are heavy black markings with white blotches towards the apex of the forewings. The underside of the forewing is similar to the upperside, but the hindwing is beautifully patterned with shades of olive-brown, white and blue. The sexes are similar, but the females tend to be larger with more rounded wings.

A range of larval foodplants are used but thistles seem to be most regularly chosen. The eggs are laid singly on the upper surface of a leaf and the larva moves to the underside to feed within a silken tent. In the later instars, the larva is more conspicuous and is often seen feeding in the open. The pupa, which is grey marked with gold, may be found hanging on the foodplant. The first painted ladies reach the British coasts in May and June, and may be seen until the end of September. Most individuals are killed off by the arrival of cold weather.

The painted lady is widespread in the three counties although numbers vary greatly from year to year. In 1980 large numbers were seen in many parts of the region, but in 1984 very few were reported from the whole of Britain, suggesting that there had been little dispersal from breeding areas in Europe and Africa. Weather systems play a major part in migrations and a favourable airflow at the appropriate time of year may give rise to a large influx of migratory butterflies.

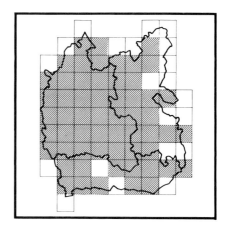

Small tortoiseshell
Aglais urticae

The small tortoiseshell is a familiar garden butterfly and is one of the first butterflies to be seen in early spring. It also occurs in a range of other habitats and is likely to be found wherever suitable patches of common nettle grow. In spring the males set up territories and will bask in the same spots for hours, usually starting at about midday. They intercept passing butterflies and when a female is encountered, a fine courtship display takes place, with the two individuals spiralling into the air. In the autumn the butterflies are only concerned with feeding before hibernation and become avid nectar feeders, especially on garden flowers such as buddleia, ice plant and Michaelmas daisies.

The upperside of the butterfly has a reddish-orange ground colour with alternate yellow and black patches along the upper edge of the forewings. The margins of all four wings are edged with blue and black lunules — the blue is more noticeable in fresh specimens. The underside is a mottled dark brown which provides excellent camouflage when the butterfly is roosting or hibernating.

Following mating, which occurs at dusk, the eggs are laid in batches under the terminal leaves of nettle plants. The females usually lay in early afternoon and will choose a patch of young nettles in a sunny situation. The larvae, which are gregarious when young, feed under a silken web which is spun around the apex of a nettle shoot. Mature larvae, which are spiny, are black and yellow in colour. They disperse before pupation, and in a garden pupae are often found in sheds or other outbuildings, well away from the nettle patch. The butterflies may be seen almost continuously from March until October, when hibernation commences. There may be a short gap in June when all the hibernating butterflies have died and before the first of the next brood have emerged.

Small tortoiseshells visit all flowery gardens in the three counties but in the countryside they occur in smaller numbers, except perhaps in years of exceptional abundance as in 1982.

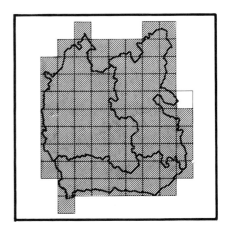

Large tortoiseshell
Nymphalis polychloros

The large tortoiseshell is now a rare butterfly in Britain — it was last recorded in any abundance in 1948. It is a woodland species and before its decline, was usually seen on the outskirts of woods, or along roads and lanes bordered by elms — the main foodplant of the species. The butterflies are elusive and fly swiftly around the tops of tall trees. However, they frequently bask on the ground in sunshine and also visit flowers and tree sap for feeding.

In appearance the butterfly is not unlike the small tortoiseshell. However, it is larger, and the ground colour is a brownish-orange with seven black blotches on each forewing rather than the six of the small tortoiseshell. The underside of the wings is mottled brown and greyish-purple.

In spring the eggs are laid in batches on small twigs of the foodplant. Elms are usually chosen, but willows and wild cherry have also been reported. The larvae feed gregariously under webs on the leaves and remain together until mature. They then fall to the ground and crawl off individually to find a pupation site. The butterflies emerge in July and August and are believed to be only on the wing for a short time before entering hibernation. After hibernation the butterflies are on the wing from early April to mid-May.

The large tortoiseshell has always been rather irregular in appearance in England and there were few places where an entomologist could guarantee seeing one every year. In many ways this observation is similar to the position with migrant species and some people believe that it is only a temporary resident in many parts of the country. In recent years there have only been sporadic records from the three counties, including sightings in the Chilterns and in the Windsor Forest area of Berkshire. Individuals have also been recorded in two separate years at a site in north Oxfordshire. However, as it is not certain whether these records are immigrants, deliberate releases or misidentifications, we are uncertain whether the large tortoiseshell is still a resident in the three counties.

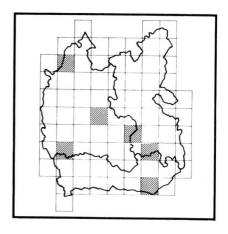

Peacock
Inachis io

The peacock is a common and welcome visitor to the garden and is often seen in good numbers in late summer, feeding avidly on flowers such as buddleia and Michaelmas daisies. It occurs in many habitats but is perhaps commonest in and around woodlands, where suitable patches of common nettle grow in sunny but sheltered situations. Peacocks emerge from hibernation on the first sunny, warm days in March. The males set up territories, often along woodland edges, and individuals can be seen interacting together, spiralling upwards into the air. The new summer brood of peacocks are mainly concerned with feeding and are attracted to large concentrations of nectar plants. They feed not only in gardens but also in woodland rides and meadows, where they are particularly fond of thistles and teasels which they often share with brimstones.

Peacocks are quite unmistakable in appearance. The ground colour of the upperside is a velvety dark red and each wing has a distinctive peacock eye marking. The colour illustration shows a butterfly with a bird-pecked eye spot. It is thought that eye spots may be a predator defence mechanism, whereby birds are deceived into pecking the eye spot rather than the real eye. The underside is almost black in colour, and in flight peacocks are seen as large, dark butterflies. The sexes are similar and not easy to distinguish.

The eggs are laid in mid-May in batches on the underside of young nettle leaves. The female chooses nettles which are growing in sheltered situations, often plants along a hedge or at the woodland edge. The spiny, black larvae live gregariously when young under a web of silk. Mature larvae leave this web and disperse to feed prior to pupation. The butterflies emerge in late July and disappear into hibernation in September. Favoured hibernation sites include hollow trees and wood piles, but they also come into sheds and houses where they are often seen fluttering at windows in warm spells during the winter.

Peacocks are common in our region and occur in good numbers in every 10 km square.

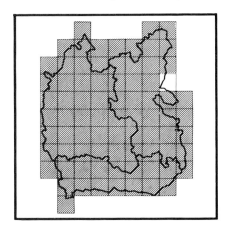

Comma
Polygonia c-album

The comma is predominantly a woodland butterfly and may be seen in sheltered rides and clearings, and along wood edges. In wooded districts commas will also come into gardens to seek nectar and are often seen sharing the buddleia bushes with other butterflies. They will bask for long periods on low vegetation but when disturbed, will fly away swiftly and are difficult to follow.

A striking feature of this butterfly's appearance is the jagged outline of the wings, which should enable easy identification. The ground colour of the upperside is a deep orange, marked with dark brown blotches, and both pairs of wings have a lighter brown border. The underside is mottled with shades of brown and there is a white comma mark in the centre of the hindwing. In the first brood a proportion of the butterflies are of a form known as *hutchinsoni*. These differ in being paler and brighter on the upperside, and paler on the underside. When in flight *hutchinsoni* commas could be confused with fritillaries.

The eggs are laid singly or in small groups on the edges of leaves of common nettle, hop or elm. The mature larvae are very distinctive with half the spiny body being a glossy white on the upper surface and the rest of the body black with heavy orange markings. The pupa is also strikingly marked with gold or silver spots and can be found suspended from the foodplant.

Commas hibernate as adults and may appear on the wing as early as March in warm spells of weather. These individuals die towards the end of May and the first brood appears in July. A later emergence occurs in September and all the butterflies have usually disappeared into hibernation by the middle of October[5].

The comma is widespread in our area and in recent years has become quite common in suitable habitats. It is interesting to note that commas were considered rarities in the first decade of this century. In the Oxford district previous to 1921 *'it was met with at long intervals and nearly always by single specimens'*[16].

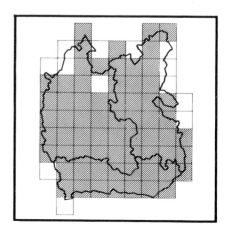

Small pearl-bordered fritillary
Boloria selene

In our region, the small pearl-bordered fritillary is a woodland butterfly, occurring in both deciduous and coniferous woodland. There is a preference for the wetter woods and the presence of rushes and ragged-robin is a feature of many *selene* sites. The butterflies have a swift and gliding flight and often congregate in warm areas within a wood where there are local concentrations of nectar plants, such as ragged-robin, bugle and marsh thistle. At night they often roost on the flowering heads of rushes.

The upperside of the small pearl-bordered fritillary is orange-brown with dark brown markings. The upper surface is brighter and darker than the similarly marked pearl-bordered fritillary, but it is the underside of the hindwings which allows positive identification. The small pearl-bordered fritillary has seven silvery 'pearls' near the hindwing border, and seven silvery cells around a central eyed cell. The pearl-bordered has the same seven 'pearls' but has only two silvery cells around the eyed cell.

Eggs are laid on or near plants of common dog-violet and marsh violet. The larvae are brown with yellowish spines and are very elusive. Most larvae hibernate after the third moult and resume feeding in the spring. The butterflies emerge in early June, usually two weeks later than pearl-bordered fritillaries. In warm summers there may be a partial second brood in August.

The small pearl-bordered fritillary is a rare butterfly in our area, being restricted to a small number of woods in Berkshire and Buckinghamshire. This attractive butterfly was probably never common in the two northerly counties and old records suggest that it was always more local than the pearl-bordered. Only one small colony was reported from Buckinghamshire in 1984. However, in Berkshire it was always the commoner of the two, and now survives mainly in the south of the county, in the wetter woods on London clay and tertiary gravels. The butterfly has also been recorded on areas of heathland adjacent to woods, such as Silchester Common.

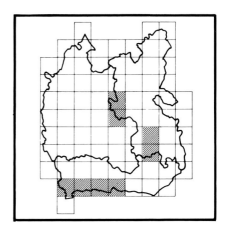

Pearl-bordered fritillary
Boloria euphrosyne

The pearl-bordered fritillary is a very local and declining species in southern England, having shown a major contraction in range over the past 100 years. The butterflies fly swiftly and gracefully in rides and clearings in large woods — particularly in areas which were cut two or three years previously. Violets, the foodplant of the larvae, usually flourish in these clearings, as do vital nectar plants such as bugle.

The upperside is a rich orange-brown with dark brown markings, and is similar, but less heavily marked than the small pearl-bordered fritillary. The females have more rounded wings and are yellower on the upperside. In both sexes the hindwing underside has seven silver 'pearls' around the border and two silver cells near the centre.

The eggs are laid on or near young common dog-violet plants. The larvae are black and spiny and may be seen feeding during the day or basking on dead leaves near the violets. They hibernate amongst leaf litter after the third moult and recommence feeding the following spring. The butterfly appears in the middle of May and flies until the middle of June.

In the early 1900s the pearl-bordered fritillary was said to *'abound in all the woods in May near Oxford'*[16]. During the same period it was said to occur in many Buckinghamshire woods[2], and the species was likewise found in a number of woods in Berkshire, often sharing the habitat with the small pearl-bordered fritillary[1]. After 1950 the pearl-bordered fritillary suffered a major decline in the Oxford district and three previously strong colonies had disappeared by 1962[17]. Similar declines were noticed throughout the region and today the butterfly is only known to occur in a single colony in the Bernwood Forest complex, where it survives in an area of mixed plantation. A major factor responsible for this decline has been the cessation of coppice management which provided the continuity of open clearings which are so vital for the survival of these butterflies.

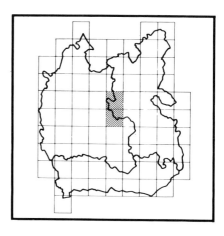

High brown fritillary
Argynnis adippe

The high brown fritillary has shown a dramatic decline in the last 30 years and is now a rare butterfly in most parts of Britain. It is essentially a woodland butterfly, occurring in areas of coppice, open rides and clearings, and scrubby fields adjacent or within the larger woodland complexes. It is a powerful flier and difficult to identify on the wing. However, it is fond of feeding on bramble, knapweed and thistle flowers, which should enable the observer to have a close view of the underside.

The butterfly is a bright orange-brown with black spots and veins. On the underside the hindwing is marked with silver spots and crescents, and inside the marginal row of silver crescents is a row of silver-pupilled red spots. These red spots are the main diagnostic feature, distinguishing the high brown from the dark green fritillary.

The eggs are laid on or near violets, and do not hatch until the following spring. The larvae feed by day on the young violet leaves and leave characteristic feeding notches in the edges of the leaves. Pupation takes place within a tent made by spinning a few leaves together. The butterflies emerge in late June or early July and are on the wing until the second week of August.

Before its decline, the high brown fritillary was widespread in the three counties. According to one observer it was the dominant fritillary in many woods up to about 1953, when it declined and disappeared from many places[18]. A number of factors may have been responsible — the felling of large deciduous woods and replanting with conifers; the ploughing of scrubby marginal land adjacent to woods; and the recent neglect of many woods with the resultant shading of violets.

Today the status of the high brown fritillary in the three counties remains uncertain. Because of the difficulty of identification, some records have been rejected. There have been no positive sightings since 1980 and so there must be a possibility that this butterfly is extinct in our area.

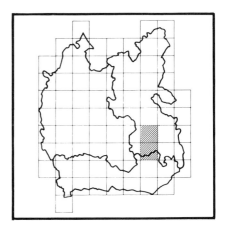

Dark green fritillary
Argynnis aglaja

Dark green fritillaries occur typically on unimproved calcareous grassland where grazing levels permit a light covering of scrub. Although these butterflies are more likely to be found on the larger tracts of downland, they can survive on much smaller patches and will even utilise open woodland if violets, the larval foodplant, are present in unshaded situations. These large, attractive butterflies are powerful fliers and are often only glimpsed in flight. They are strongly attracted to thistles and knapweeds for nectar, but only pause briefly to feed and are not easy to observe closely.

The upperside of the wings is a rich tawny orange marked with black. The underside of the hindwing is green at the basal area with large silver spots. There is an additional row of silver spots near the margin. The sexes are similar except that the females tend to be yellower in colour and more heavily marked.

The eggs are laid singly or near the leaves of either hairy violet or one of the two dog-violets, *Viola riviniana* and *V. reichenbachiana*. The newly hatched larva overwinters at the base of the plant and does not start feeding until the following spring. The larvae feed during the day and are active in sunshine. They pupate in a loose spun cocoon among grasses and leaves. The butterflies emerge in early July and are on the wing until mid-August.

The dark green fritillary is the commonest of our fritillaries and still occurs at a number of places in the Chilterns, Berkshire Downs and on Oxfordshire limestone. They have also been recorded in some of the larger woods and can thrive in young conifer plantations. However, conditions in these plantations usually become too shaded after seven to ten years and, as in the case of Bernwood Forest, the butterfly gradually disappears. The dark green fritillary has also declined on some of the calcareous sites, particularly since 1980. As so little is known about the ecology of this butterfly, it is difficult to know the full reasons for this decline.

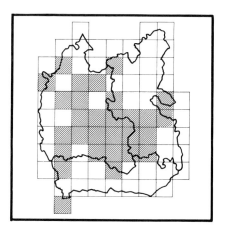

Silver-washed fritillary
Argynnis paphia

Like the other woodland fritillaries, the silver-washed fritillary is a declining species in southern England. It only occurs in the larger areas of woodland, where there are blocks of mature timber trees and flowery rides or edges. The butterflies have a strong sweeping flight and are frequent visitors to bramble and thistle blossoms. They often congregate on these plants in sunny clearings and rides.

This attractive butterfly is the largest of the British fritillaries and has distinctive long forewings. The upperside of the male is a bright orange-brown, marked with black spots and streaks across the forewings. The female is slightly larger and the forewings have a paler ground colour, marked with larger black spots. The hindwings are darker and have a greenish tint. The underside of the hindwing in both sexes is a mixture of pale pink and green with silver washed in irregular bands.

Unlike the other fritillaries, the eggs are laid on the trunks of trees. The female flies low down near the bases of trees and looks for a suitable clump of violets. She then flies up to a height of nearly two metres and deposits an egg into a crevice in the bark of the chosen tree. After hatching the larva immediately hibernates in the bark, and the following spring descends to locate the violet plants. The larvae are very active and usually wander off to pupate away from the foodplant. The butterflies appear on the wing in July and August.

The silver-washed fritillary can still be found in a number of the larger woods in our region, but is rarely seen in good numbers. Colonies are thinly scattered in the Chilterns, and the butterfly still survives in some of its old haunts in north-west Oxfordshire and south Berkshire. The silver-washed has not declined as dramatically as the other woodland fritillaries because of its ability to tolerate shadier conditions. However, it is known to have disappeared from several woods near Oxford where coniferisation has resulted in the loss of suitable habitat.

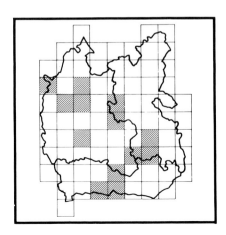

Marsh fritillary
Eurodryas aurinia

The marsh fritillary occurs in three distinct habitats in our region; wet herb-rich meadows, calcareous grassland and open woodland rides. However, suitable habitat is becoming increasingly scarce and so the marsh fritillary is now a rare butterfly. The males are active in sunshine, although they tend only to make short flights between basking or feeding on nectar plants. The females are particularly sluggish and can be found sitting on low vegetation.

The upperside of the wings is reddish-brown with straw yellow bands and black markings. The undersides are pale versions of the uppersides. The butterflies are very distinctive and easily distinguished from the other small fritillaries.

The eggs are laid in batches of up to 500 on the underside of a leaf of devil's-bit scabious. The young larvae feed gregariously beneath a silken web at the base of the plant, and hibernate after the third moult. In March the black and spiny larvae can be found in small groups basking on the plants. During the final instar they disperse from the webs and feed solitarily until pupation. The butterflies appear in late May and

the flight season lasts about one month.

The marsh fritillary is very scarce in the three counties — indeed there is only one strong colony which exists on a nature reserve in Oxfordshire. The other post-1975 records represent either small, ephemeral colonies or single vagrants. In exceptionally warm summers, such as 1976, adults occasionally stray several miles from an established colony. Small colonies still exist on the Berkshire Downs although very few butterflies are seen each year. Before 1950 the marsh fritillary was more widespread. It was common in several widely separated stations near Oxford[16, 19], and in Buckinghamshire it was found locally *'in some of the marshy hollows among the Chiltern Hills, and in some seasons on the tops of hills, where scabious is growing'*[2]. Today there are very few colonies in Buckinghamshire, and one woodland colony which existed until the mid-1970s was destroyed by heavy equipment transporting timber and obliterating the foodplant.

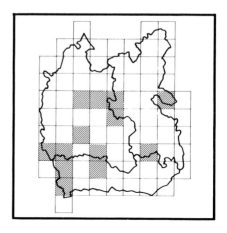

Speckled wood
Pararge aegeria

Speckled woods are one of our commonest woodland butterflies and they may be the only butterfly seen in shaded neglected coppice or mature plantations. They also fly along hedgerows and leafy lanes, particularly in damp places. Speckled woods are fascinating butterflies to watch. The males perch on vegetation in dappled sunlight, from which they make short flights as if patrolling a territory. They have frequent skirmishes with other males and pairs can be seen spiralling upwards together. They feed predominantly on honeydew, particularly in the early part of the year. However, the summer broods can be seen at flowers and also enjoy feeding on blackberries.

The upperside of the wings is a deep chocolate brown patterned with cream spots. These spots can vary in size and colour, and some contain eye spots. The underside of the forewing is similar to that of the upperside, but the hindwing is a mottled brown and cream with submarginal eye spots. The males are smaller than females and have more pointed forewings.

The eggs are laid on a range of grasses, but only on those which are growing in shaded situations.

The larvae feed up quickly, enabling a succession of broods during the summer. The butterfly is believed to overwinter either as a larva or a pupa which produces two overlapping, spring flight periods — the first in April and May, and the second from May to June. The next generation emerges in July and August and in some years the butterflies may be seen until early November.

With the exception of parts of east Buckinghamshire, the speckled wood is widespread in our region and occurs in most woods. However, this is a result of a dramatic expansion which occurred in the 1940s and 1950s. In the Oxford District during the early years of this century speckled woods were said to be *'singularly scarce, and only found with certainty in one of the northern woods . . .* '[16]. By 1947 they were considered common in the Oxford District[20], and this pattern of expansion of range has been repeated over much of England and Wales.

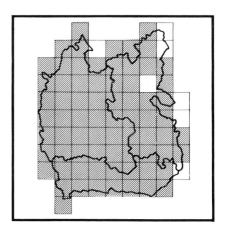

Wall
Lasiommata megera

The wall occurs in a variety of habitats — unimproved calcareous grassland, disused quarries, woodland rides and edges, roadsides and even gardens, usually preferring the warm, sheltered spots within these habitats. The butterflies are active in sunshine and make short flights between basking with open wings on warm surfaces such as stony pathways and banks. When basking, walls often adopt a distinctive pose with one forewing dropping lower than the other, giving a rather lopsided impression.

The upperside of the wings is an orange-brown colour patterned with dark lines and markings. There is a prominent white-pupilled eye spot near the apex of each forewing and a row of smaller spots along the margins of the hindwings. The males have a stripe of dark scent scales crossing the forewings, while the females are larger and paler and have more rounded wings. The underside of the hindwings is greyish marked with dark lines and eye spots. This patterning provides superb camouflage when the butterfly is at rest on a stone surface. Walls have been confused with small fritillaries but the presence of eye spots on the wall is diagnostic.

The eggs are laid singly on grass blades or exposed roots in warm sheltered spots such as rabbit scrapes or bank overhangs. In woodland rides and hedges, the eggs are laid on grasses which are sheltered by shrubs. The larvae feed on a range of grasses and the summer brood overwinters in the third instar. They continue to feed on mild days throughout the winter and complete their growth by mid-April. The butterflies emerge in late May and can be seen for about five weeks. The summer brood is on the wing in July and August and usually more individuals are seen. In warm seasons there may be a small third brood in October.

The wall is widely but thinly spread in the three counties and possibly occurs in every 10 km square. They are rarely seen in any numbers and in some seasons are quite scarce.

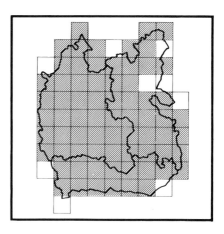

Marbled white
Melanarqia qalathea

The marbled white is a widespread and locally abundant species in parts of England and south Wales, occurring on unimproved, rough grassland. Chalk and limestone hills support the strongest colonies, but the butterfly is not necessarily restricted to calcareous soils. Colonies can also be found in open woodland rides, along railway embankments and even roadside verges. The butterflies are usually gregarious and a patch of sheltered limestone grassland near Oxford one hectare in extent supported over 500 individuals in 1980. They have a slow flapping flight and are avid nectar feeders in sunshine. They are often seen on thistles, knapweeds, marjoram and scabious flowers.

The butterflies are very distinctive in appearance and cannot be confused with any of the other 'browns'. The upperside of the wings has a whitish ground colour with robust black markings. The underside markings are similar but paler than the upperside, and there is a row of eye spots near the margin of the hindwing. The female is larger than the male, and has browner markings on the underside — this difference is par-

ticularly apparent when a mating pair is seen.

The eggs are laid at random in areas of long grass, and the newly emerged larvae go immediately into hibernation. Feeding commences on warm days in January and February, on grasses such as sheep's-fescue and Yorkshire-fog. By June the larvae are ready to pupate and in late June or early July, the butterflies emerge, with the flight period lasting about three weeks.

The marbled white is widespread in the three counties, with the exception of north-east Buckinghamshire and south-east Berkshire. In fact, they are scarce or absent to the north and east of our region. Marbled whites are most numerous on calcareous soils, and in High Wycombe they extend right into the town, occurring on waste ground completely surrounded by housing, and on rough banks alongside playing fields[21].

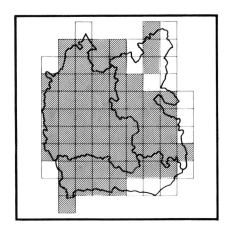

Grayling
Hipparchia semele

The grayling occurs on dry, well-drained soils in scattered colonies throughout the British Isles. Heathland, chalk and limestone grassland, coastal dunes and cliffs, can all support colonies, but in our area the grayling is now restricted to the Berkshire heathlands. They require sheltered and relatively hot situations and are often found where the ground is bare in places and the vegetation sparse. The grayling is slightly larger than the meadow brown and can be readily identified by observing its behaviour patterns. The butterfly flies swiftly for short distances and then settles on a suitable spot with wings closed and the hindwing completely covering the forewing.

The upper surface of the wings is brown with pale yellow and orange bands containing eye spots. These bands and spots are more pronounced in the female than in the male. The forewing underside is orange-brown with two white-pupilled black spots. The hindwing underside is greyish, mottled with brown and white, which provides a marvellous camouflage when the butterfly is at rest on a tree trunk, rock or gravel.

The eggs are laid singly on grass blades and a range of grass species is used. The larvae feed at night and hibernate over the winter. Pupation takes place just below the surface of the soil. The butterflies emerge late July and are on the wing until early September.

In the three counties, the grayling is confined to acidic soils in Berkshire. The butterfly flourishes on a number of the heathy commons and woods such as Silchester and Bucklebury, and on the patches of heathland in the Sandhurst and Crowthorne area. Graylings often fly amongst birches on heathland and they are particularly well camouflaged when resting on birch bark. In hot summers they may stray from the breeding areas and in 1976, for example, single specimens were recorded at a number of sites, including Bradfield in Berkshire, and Bix Bottom in Oxfordshire. There are old records of breeding colonies on calcareous soils in the Chilterns, such as at Watlington Hill[4], but there have been no confirmed sightings since 1980.

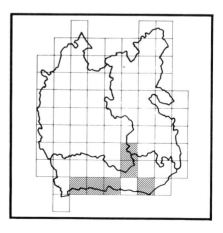

Hedge brown
Pyronia tithonus

The hedge brown, sometimes known as the gatekeeper, is a widespread and common butterfly which, as its name suggests, is often found flying alongside hedges. Field and woodland edges, roadside verges and grassy tracks, are typical places where you would expect to find this butterfly. In the right sheltered situations, hedge browns can be seen in large numbers and are attracted to concentrations of nectar plants. On downland they often use marjoram as a nectar source, whilst in woodland rides brambles, thistles and yellow composite flowers are popular sources. In Bernwood Forest groups of 30-50 individuals were seen feeding on common fleabane and common ragwort in 1984.

The males have a rich tawny upperside with broad, dark brown borders and a dark brown bar on the forewings. The female is larger, lighter tan in colour and does not have a brown bar on the forewing. Both sexes also have a black spot with two white dots on the forewing, and a smaller spot at the lower angle of the hindwing. The underside of the hindwing is mottled brown with several small white dots — providing ex-

cellent camouflage when roosting. The number and size of eye spots can vary a good deal but the presence of two white pupils on the underside eye spot is useful for distinguishing the hedge brown from a meadow brown.

The eggs are laid singly on a variety of grasses in lightly shaded places such as beneath shrubs. The larvae feed at night until October, when hibernation begins. In spring they recommence feeding and by mid-June they are fully grown and ready to pupate. The butterflies emerge in July, usually about three weeks after the meadow brown, and remain on the wing until mid-September.

Hedge browns are one of the commonest butterflies in our region, being both widespread and abundant. However, in the intensively farmed areas where many hedges have been removed, the total number of colonies has almost certainly declined.

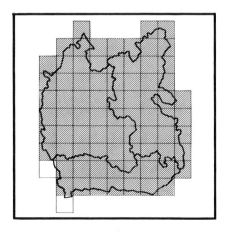

Meadow brown
Maniola jurtina

The meadow brown is one of the commonest butterflies in Great Britain, occurring on almost every area of rough grassland and is only absent from improved leys and manicured lawns. Downland, unimproved hay meadows, heathland, woodland rides and roadside verges can all support strong populations of this butterfly. Meadow browns have a distinctive, rather lazy flight and are one of the few butterflies which will fly in dull conditions. They are often seen in large numbers and, like the hedge brown, are avid nectar feeders. A bramble patch can be covered with several dozen meadow browns — other favourites are marjoram, knapweed, field scabious and wild privet.

The males have a dark brown upperside with a white-centred black spot on the forewing. There is often a small patch of orange near the eye spot. The females have a much larger patch of orange on the upperside and more prominent eye spots. The forewing underside in both sexes has a pale orange ground colour with a dark brown border and black spot with a single white pupil. The hindwing underside is patterned with light and dark brown.

Eggs are laid singly on blades of grass, sometimes where the grass is tall but not dense — but they have also been observed laying in hay meadows after the hay crop has been removed. The larvae feed on a range of different grasses and overwinter in grass tussocks, although still feeding whenever the weather is mild. Pupation takes place low down among the grass stems and the butterflies emerge in mid-June. The flight season is long and will extend to early October in some years.

Although not numerous in gardens or suburban areas, meadow browns are one of the most widespread and abundant butterflies in the three counties. Indeed at ideal sites where the grass grows tall but not too densely, such as open woodland rides or urban waste ground, the butterfly can be seen in enormous numbers. In the intensively farmed areas of the region, small colonies exist along field margins and hedges, and roadside verges.

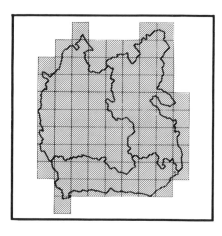

Small heath
Coenonympha pamphilus

The small heath is a common grassland butterfly, occurring in a range of habitats from chalk downland to heath and open woodland rides, to roadside and railway banks and disturbed waste ground in urban areas. The butterfly has a slow flight and can fly close to the ground, an ability which enables it to survive on windswept sites. It does not fly very far and spends much of its time resting on grass stems or flower heads. A range of flowers are visited for nectar, including tormentil, knapweeds and devil's-bit scabious.

The small heath is the smallest of our 'brown' butterflies. It always settles with its wings closed and its dull colouring makes it easily overlooked. The upperside of the wings is a rich yellow-ochre with a brownish fringe at the margins. There is a small black spot near the apex of the fore-wings. The underside of the fore-wing is a deeper orange-brown than the upperside, and has a yellow-ringed, black eye spot. The hindwing is greyish with a darker patch near the body, which provides excellent camouflage when the butterfly is at rest. The female is generally larger and does not have the dark marginal borders on the upperside.

The eggs are laid singly on grass blades, usually on the finer-leaved species such as bents and fescues. The larvae from the later summer brood overwinter in this stage and occasionally feed during spells of mild weather. The pupae, which are green with brown markings on the wing cases, can be found attached to a grass stem. Small heaths are double brooded in our region, with the first brood flying from May until July and the second brood in August and September.

The small heath is widespread in the three counties but is nothing like as prominent or numerous as the meadow or hedge brown. Colonies tend to be small and are easily overlooked. Very little is known about the ecology of this butterfly, and the exact sequence of broods requires elucidation.

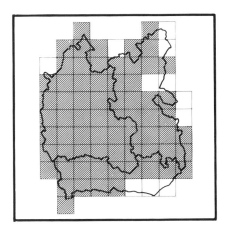

Ringlet
Aphantopus hyperantus

The ringlet occurs in sheltered areas of rough grassland, such as that found at woodland edges, in woodland rides and glades, or along sheltered roadside verges. The butterfly has a weak flight and is often seen fluttering slowly among long grasses in shady, damp places. A range of flowers is visited for nectar, including thistles, common fleabane and brambles, with the latter being the preferred food source.

Although ringlets often fly with meadow browns, which they closely match in size, they may be distinguished on the wing by their much darker colouration. The upperside of the wings is dark chocolate brown with white fringes. The females tend to be larger and paler in colour. The undersides of both wings have very prominent white-pupilled eye spots which are ringed with yellow, which gives rise to the butterfly's common name.

The eggs are dropped to the ground in areas of long grass and the larvae probably feed on a number of grass species. Overwintering is in the larval stage and the larvae feed during the winter whenever conditions are mild. By June the larvae are fully grown and the pupa is formed on the ground at the base of grasses. The butterflies emerge in early July and will fly until the middle of August.

The ringlet is widely distributed in the three counties, but does not occur in the same numbers as some of the other common brown species. The populations tend to be small and well-defined and so colonies may be overlooked on large sites. The butterfly is absent from open heathland and exposed downland. Ringlets were very common in the hot summers of 1975 and 1976, but numbers declined sharply in 1977. It is likely that some degree of dampness is important in the larval development, and so hot, dry weather in late summer may cause high larval mortality. Fortunately numbers have since increased and in 1984, ringlets were a common roadside verge butterfly in many parts of the three counties.

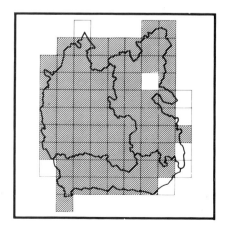

Rare migrants, vagrants and accidental species

Several species of butterfly have been recorded over the years which do not breed regularly in our region, but which might conceivably be encountered at some time in the future. The interpretation of records of these rarities is often difficult. Many are not supported by a photograph or a specimen and so there can be some doubt about identification. In recent years live butterfly stock has been readily available commercially and some records probably refer to escapes or releases of bred stock. In this category come two recent large copper (*Lycaena dispar*) records from Buckinghamshire. There is a rumour that the butterfly once bred on Otmoor[16], where its foodplant still grows, but in all probability it has not occurred naturally in the region for at least 200 years. There are two Oxfordshire records of swallowtail (*Papilio machaon*) in recent years which could either be releases or continental vagrants.

Several records of the pale clouded yellow (*Colias hyale*) were received in 1983, but as there is the possibility of confusion with the *helice* form of *C. croceus* these records may be mistaken. There is also the possibility of confusion with the much rarer Berger's clouded yellow (*C. australis*), which is very similar to *C. hyale*.

Regular, but infrequent migrants, include Camberwell beauty (*Nymphalis antiopa*), monarch (*Danaus plexippus*) and Bath white (*Pontia daplidice*). The glamorous Camberwell beauty is seen in ones or twos most years. It migrates from continental Europe and often feeds in large gardens. Monarchs are seen about once per decade with the most recent record being from Buckinghamshire in 1981[26]. This American butterfly has recently colonized the Canary Islands where milkweed, its larval foodplant, grows in quantity. Milkweed is a garden plant in Cornwall and so there is a possibility that monarchs might breed there one day. Bath whites, which are very similar in appearance to female orange tips, were seen much more regularly a century ago than they are now. The most recent record is from Buckinghamshire in 1969.

Two very rare migrants for which there are single records in our region are the Queen of Spain fritillary (*Argynnis lathonia*), recorded from Berkshire in 1867, and the Weaver's fritillary (*Boloria dia*), recorded from Berkshire in 1837[4].

Recent rumours that the large blue (*Maculinea arion*) still survives in the Cotswolds must be treated with scepticism. However, it is possible that an eighteenth century record from Cliveden, Buckinghamshire is genuine. Nineteenth century records of the heath fritillary (*Mellicta athalia*) from Bagley Wood near Oxford cannot be authenticated without specimens, but as their favoured coppiced-woodland habitat was present the records could be genuine.

The chances of seeing any of these rare species is very remote. If they are encountered it is useful either to take a photograph or to make detailed notes on markings in order to make sure that the record is genuine and accepted by all.

Colour Plates

PLATE 1
Small skipper
Essex skipper
Silver-spotted skipper
Large skipper
Dingy skipper
Grizzled skipper

PLATE 2
Wood white
Clouded yellow
Brimstone
Large white
Small white
Green-veined white

PLATE 3
Orange tip
Green hairstreak
Brown hairstreak
Purple hairstreak
White-letter hairstreak
Black hairstreak

PLATE 4
Small copper
Small blue
Silver-studded blue
Brown argus
Common blue
Chalkhill blue

PLATE 5
Adonis blue
Holly blue
Duke of Burgundy
White admiral
Purple emperor
Red admiral

PLATE 6
Painted lady
Small tortoiseshell
Large tortoiseshell
Peacock
Comma
Small pearl-bordered fritillary

PLATE 7
Pearl-bordered fritillary
High brown fritillary
Dark green fritillary
Silver-washed fritillary
Marsh fritillary
Speckled wood

PLATE 8
Wall
Marbled white
Grayling
Meadow brown, Hedge brown
Small heath
Ringlet

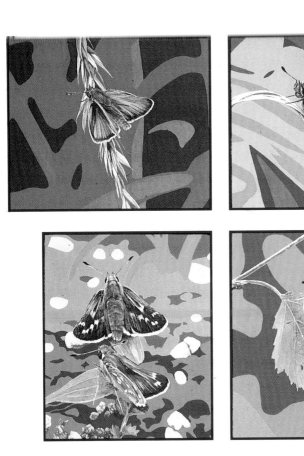

Small skipper ♂	Essex skipper
Silver-spotted skipper, ♀ *upper*, ♂ *lower*	Large skipper
Dingy skipper	Grizzled skipper

Plate 1

Wood white, ♂ *left*, ♀ *right*   Clouded yellow
Brimstone ♀   Large white
Small white   Green-veined white

Plate 2

Orange tip♂   Green hairstreak
Brown hairstreak♀   Purple hairstreak ♀
White-letter hairstreak   Black hairstreak

Plate 3

Small copper
Silver-studded blue♂
Common blue♂

Small blue ♂
Brown argus
Chalkhill blue, ♂ *left*, ♀ *right*

Plate 4

Adonis blue ♂   Holly blue ♀
Duke of Burgundy   White admiral
Purple emperor ♂   Red admiral

Plate 5

Painted lady   Small tortoiseshell
Large tortoiseshell   Peacock
Comma   Small pearl-bordered fritillary ♀

Plate 6

Pearl-bordered fritillary   High brown fritillary   ♂ *foreground*
Dark green fritillary   Silver-washed fritillary ♂
Marsh fritillary   Speckled wood

Plate 7

Wall ♂   Marbled white ♂
Grayling   Meadow brown *left*, Hedge brown *right*
Small heath   Ringlet

Plate 8

Nectar and larval plants

Alder buckthorn *Frangula alnus*
Bitter vetch *Lathyrus montanus*
Black medick *Medicago lupulina*
Blackthorn *Prunus spinosa*
Bluebell *Hyacinthoides non-scripta*
Bramble *Rubus* sp.
Buckthorn *Rhamnus catharticus*
Bugle *Ajuga reptans*
Cocks-foot *Dactylis glomerata*
Common bird's-foot trefoil *Lotus corniculatus*
Common dog-violet *Viola riviniana*
Common fleabane *Pulicaria dysenterica*
Common nettle *Urtica dioica*
Common ragwort *Senecio jacobaea*
Common restharrow *Ononis repens*
Common rock-rose *Helianthemum nummularium*
Common sorrel *Rumex acetosa*
Cow parsley *Anthriscus sylvestris*
Cowslip *Primula veris*
Creeping cinquefoil *Potentilla reptans*
Creeping soft-grass *Holcus mollis*
Cuckoo flower *Cardamine pratensis*
Dandelion *Taraxacum* sp.
Devils-bit scabious *Succisa pratensis*
Dogwood *Cornus sanguinea*
Dove's-foot cranes-bill *Geranium molle*
Dwarf thistle *Cirsium acaule*
Dyer's greenweed *Genista tinctoria*
Early dog-violet *Viola reichenbachiana*
Elm *Ulmus* spp
False-brome *Brachypodium sylvaticum*
Field scabious *Knautia arvensis*
Garlic mustard *Alliaria petiolata*

Goat willow *Salix caprea*
Gorse *Ulex europaeus*
Hawkbit *Leontodon* spp
Hairy violet *Viola hirta*
Hedge mustard *Sisymbrium officinale*
Hogweed *Heracleum sphondylium*
Holly *Ilex aquifolium*
Honeysuckle *Lonicera periclymenum*
Hop *Humulus lupulus*
Ivy *Hedera helix*
Kidney vetch *Anthyllis vulneraria*
Knapweed *Centaurea* spp
Lucerne *Medicago sativa*
Marjoram *Origanum vulgare*
Marsh thistle *Cirsium palustre*
Marsh violet *Viola palustris*
Meadow vetchling *Lathyrus pratensis*
Oak *Quercus* spp
Primrose *Primula vulgaris*
Purple moor-grass *Molinia caerulea*
Ragged-robin *Lychnis flos-cuculi*
Red clover *Trifolium pratense*
Sheep's-fescue *Festuca ovina*
Sheep's sorrel *Rumex acetosella*
Teasel *Dipsacus fullonum*
Tor-grass *Brachypodium pinnatum*
Tormentil *Potentilla erecta*
Wild cherry *Prunus avium*
Wild privet *Ligustrum vulgare*
Wild strawberry *Fragaria vesca*
Wood spurge *Euphorbia amygdaloides*
Yorkshire-fog *Holcus lanatus*

Bibliography

1 Berkshire Victoria County History. University of London Institute of Historical Research
2 Buckinghamshire Victoria County History. University of London Institute of Historical Research
3 Oxfordshire Victoria County History Vol. 5. University of London Institute of Historical Research
4 Bowen, H. J. M. (1979) Butterflies of Berkshire, Buckinghamshire and Oxfordshire *Trans. Newbury District Field Club* 12, 61 – 72
5 Heath, J., Pollard, E., and Thomas, J. (1984) Atlas of Butterflies in Britain and Ireland. Viking
6 Goodden, R. (1978) British butterflies, David and Charles
7 Howarth, T. G. (1973) South's British Butterflies. Warne
8 Carter, W. A. C. (1958) Butterfly Collecting in the Beaconsfield District. *Jnl. Middle Thames Nat. Hist. Soc.* 4 – 9
9 Rothschild, M. and Farrell, C. (1983) The Butterfly Gardener. Michael Joseph
10 Oates, M. (1985) Garden plants for butterflies. Brian Masterton and Associates
11 Newman, L. H. (1967) Create a butterfly garden. John Baker
12 Ansorge, E. (1969) The Macrolepidoptera of Buckinghamshire. Bucks Archaeological Society
13 Peachey, C. A. (1983) White-letter hairstreak survey *News Br. Butterfly Conser. Soc.* 30, 21 – 4
14 Thomas, J. A. (undated) The Black Hairstreak Conservation Report. Institute of Terrestrial Ecology.
15 Porter, K. (1984) Brambles, bricks and bugs. *News Br. Butterfly Conser. Soc.* 33, 27 – 33
16 Walker, J. J. (1926) The Natural History of the Oxford District. O.U.P.
17 Ainley, R. G. (1962) Butterflies in the Oxford District, 1961. *Ent. Record* 74, 65 – 6
18 Robertson, T. S. (1979) *personal communication*
19 Bretherton, R. F. (1940) A list of the macro-lepidoptera of the Oxford District. *Proc. Ashmol. Nat. Hist. Soc.* 1939, 25 – 70
20 Emmet, A. M. (1948) Second supplement to the list of macrolepidoptera of the Oxford District *Proc. Ashmol. Nat. Hist. Soc.* 1941 – 7, 47 – 55
21 Grout-Smith, T. (1984) Surveys past and future. *Newsletter 5 Upper Thames Branch Br. Butterfly Conser. Soc.*, 6
22 Habitat Survey (1978 – 79, 1981), Berkshire, Buckinghamshire and Oxfordshire Naturalists' Trust
23 Nature Conservation in Great Britain (1984) Nature Conservancy Council
24 Knight, R. and Campbell, J. M. (1982) An Atlas of Oxfordshire butterflies. Occasional Paper No 2. Oxfordshire County Council, Dept. of Museum Services
25 Hall, M. L. (1981) Butterfly monitoring scheme. Instructions for independent recorders. Institute of Terrestrial Ecology, Monks Wood Experimental Station, Abbots Ripton, Huntingdon, Cambs.
26 Bretherton, R. F. and Chalmers-Hunt, J. M. (1982) The Immigration of Lepidoptera to the British Isles in 1981. *Ent. Rec.* 94, 141 – 46

Conservation Societies

Many people obtain great pleasure from their interest in butterflies and it is possible to enhance this pleasure by joining one of the relevant conservation societies where like-minded people meet together. By joining one of the societies mentioned below it will prove possible both to attend guided tours and so become familiar with all of the butterflies, and to make a positive and important contribution to butterfly conservation in our region.

The British Butterfly Conservation Society (BBCS) is dedicated to furthering the cause of butterfly conservation. There is an Upper Thames Branch, covering the three counties, which holds regular indoor meetings and guided field trips in the summer. Details of the Society may be obtained from BBCS Membership Secretary, 19 Corner Close, Wellington, Somerset TA21 8QE.

The Berkshire, Buckinghamshire and Oxfordshire Naturalists' Trust (BBONT) is dedicated to the conservation of all wildlife in our region. It manages more than 80 nature reserves, accessible to members, which support nearly all of the region's butterflies. Details may be obtained from the Membership Secretary, BBONT, 3 Church Cowley Road, Rose Hill, Oxford OX4 3JR.

Butterfly records can be sent to any of the three county museums:

BERKSHIRE: Museum and Art Gallery, Blagrave Street, Reading RG1 1QL

BUCKINGHAMSHIRE: County Museum, Church Street, Aylesbury HP2 2QP

OXFORDSHIRE: County Museum, Fletchers House, Woodstock, OX7 1JH